Lots

Clive Emson

www.newgeneration-publishing.com

New Generation Publishing

DEDICATION

To Sue, without whom I could never have achieved my dreams and to my amazing family and many close friends who have been so supportive over the challenging past three years

ACKNOWLEDGEMENTS

My thanks to Sarah Sturt for editing and guiding me through the process and Steve Ashman for his patience with sorting the computer every time I encountered an entirely avoidable problem.

DISCLAIMER

The true events and conversations in this book have been recounted to the best of my ability and scope of my memory and made in good faith, but may differ from other parties' recollections .

WARNING

I was lucky enough to have lived during the pre-woke period, so anyone who is easily offended, or think they should be offended on behalf of someone else who does not give a damn – please do us both a favour and regift the book to somebody with a sense of a humour, preferably before reading it.

CONTENTS

FOREWORD

It was about four years ago, in 2019, that I was reminiscing on how the sixteen-year-old who, in the words of his schoolmaster, "was totally unemployable" managed to be sitting on the terrace of his frontline villa in bright sunshine on the Costa del Sol, without a care in the world.

On many occasions, especially following an after-dinner speech, people have suggested that I should write a book, something which I have always taken with a pinch, if not packet, of salt!

In that balmy heat, I was considering what to do with my time, having now completely handed over the responsibility of running the business, and I decided to start recording a few anecdotes for the benefit and possible amusement of my four grandchildren. This quickly turned into a mission to write a book that I imagined would take a few weeks to complete. How wrong I was!

Life intervened when Sue became very unwell and following her passing I too was diagnosed with cancer, which took well over a year to defeat, during which time the enthusiasm for a vanity project was not only on the back burner, but nowhere near the cooker.

However, life has now taken a more structured, if totally different, direction and allowed me the time and enthusiasm to revive the project. I do hope you will enjoy reading it as much as I have enjoyed recording my thoughts and memories of the past seventy years.

CHAPTER 1

EARLY DAYS

I was born on 29 August 1946 in Birmingham where my parents, Jack and Jane Emson, were living at the time. I made my appearance five years after my brother Colin.

My mother was an only child and my father was from a larger family but, for reasons we will never know, fell out with them when he married and from then on, they did not feature in his life.

Father had been a senior administrator at the London Fire Brigade during the Blitz, helping to ensure that the right people had the right equipment needed to handle the catastrophic bombing of the city. He seldom spoke of his war years but, like so many, the horrors of death and destruction stayed with him for a very long time.

After the war he joined the Midlands fire service as a senior administrator, moving to a similar and more senior post with Kent Fire Brigade when I was still very young.

My first memories are from when we lived at 25 Allington Way in Maidstone, a new three-bedroom semi-detached house on the outskirts of town. Allington Way was, in those days, a cul-de-sac of probably no more than fifty properties and within a few hundred yards of open farmland and Bluebell Wood, where we would go for walks and play cowboys and Indians. This area has now been built on and forms part of a large housing complex that's been developed over the years.

My mother was a larger-than-life character with a ready wit who was always the life and soul of the party. A self-taught accountant by profession, she stayed at home until I went to school.

I would catch the bus to my primary school, Brunswick House, which was about three miles away. Father would come with me and continue into town and then catch another bus to Tovil, where the headquarters of Kent Fire Brigade remain to this day.

On Saturday mornings I used to go with him to his office and amuse myself by getting lost in the massive grounds of the manor house and attempting to play snooker on the full-size table. What patience father had. An upright man who rarely swore and never lost his temper, he was the archetypal gentleman – always polite, always smartly dressed.

When I was eight, we moved to a large Victorian house on the London Road, less than a mile from Maidstone town centre. Set in three-quarters of an acre, it had a tennis court, a sunken rose garden and an orchard.

Mother was by then working as a private secretary and bookkeeper to the senior partner of a well-respected, second-generation firm of chartered accountants. I always remember her as a hard worker with boundless energy, someone who enjoyed life to the full. She would partner my father at the bridge table and was an accomplished piano player and ballroom dancer.

The fact that I was dyslexic meant that I had little prospect of passing the 11+ exam, which would have enabled me to join my brother at Maidstone Grammar School where he went after attending The Cedars, a private prep school. My parents were advised by Mr Peters, the headmaster, that Colin was so bright he would be better off at the grammar school where the teaching standards were higher – rubbish advice that my parents accepted in good faith and for which my brother has never really forgiven them. He had a tough time, being bullied for being 'posh' and eventually left at sixteen, and to this day I am not sure whether it was his decision or the school's. Probably a bit of both.

As many in a similar position will appreciate, growing up in the shadow of a bright, talented sibling five years my senior was hard. He played musical instruments, won talent shows with his singing and, of course, was allowed to do all the things I wanted to do but was deemed too young.

He, on the other hand, rather resented that mother and father appeared easier going on me, a familiar gripe with many firstborn. I put it down to the fact that parents have expectations of the first child that are often unachievable and possibly unreasonable. By the time the second is born they have learned the error of their ways. Imagine how cushy it must be like for the third and fourth child! Just a theory of mine and no doubt an overgeneralisation, but you get the gist.

For me, constant frustration was the norm and striving to be noticed without being a pest proved an uphill struggle. My mother and brother enjoyed a good argument and would say the most horrible things to each other, which were promptly forgotten within hours. Mainly because of those memories, I try not to be too argumentative – which of course is not difficult when you're right most of the time anyway! I have never understood the phrase 'I didn't mean it.' Surely, if you said horrible, hurtful things, you must have thought them?

Soon after we moved to London Road my mother's parents joined us. My grandfather was a belligerent old bugger but he had a heart of gold. I was definitely his favourite and I still treasure the silver Stock Exchange boxing club cup he won when he was younger and bequeathed to me in his will.

Grandad hadn't had an easy life, but his quick wit saw him through. Once I was upstairs on the bus coming back from town when I heard him on the lower deck having a bit of an altercation with the conductor. Apparently, Grandad rang the bell for the request stop and the bus conductor shouted, 'You mustn't ring the bell – that's my job,' to which Grandad replied, 'Your job? Your job? It's woman's work' and as he got off, rang the bell again for the driver to proceed. I stayed out of the way upstairs and got off at the next stop.

My grandmother, on the other hand, was a gentle soul, riddled with arthritis for as long as I could remember, bent over in constant pain, which she bore bravely. I could understand why they moved in with us but at that young age, the dynamics of the family were somewhat strained at times.

On the whole, however, I remember my childhood as a happy one. I had my bike, which was everything to me, my local friends and some schoolfriends always close by. There was more laughter than tears. Dad enjoyed his garden and I lived at No. 37 from the age of eight until I got married. In the last six months before we wed, Sue moved in too and she and Mother loved each other to bits.

The house was always full of people. Mother used to 'adopt' the articled clerks from her office and they would often come round for drinks and a chat with Mrs E. Some years later, I was on a ski lift when the woman next to me said,

'Had it not been for your mother, I wouldn't be married to my husband.'

I wasn't sure who she was and said, 'I think you have me confused me with somebody else.' However, it appeared that when an articled clerk was considering getting married, Mrs E had to meet the young lady in question to give her seal of approval. Diana became a good friend and her husband, David (aka the young articled clerk) later worked for me when he retired.

Such was the force of Mother's personality, influence and the high respect in which her judgement was held, that the many young people from her office and, indeed, friends of mine who were privileged to be part of her life, often came to our house for sage advice, usually about a latest flame who was proving elusive.

Father suffered from chronic emphysema brought on by smoking untipped Players cigarettes and retired from Kent Fire Brigade on medical grounds in his early fifties. Once he had recovered and the medication took effect, he helped my mother, who was by then working full-time as the company accountant for my brother's hugely successful business in London.

Father was on the parole board at Maidstone Prison, president of the Maidstone Club and an experienced bridge player. He also did the clerking for my auction rooms in Hythe where we held monthly sales on a Saturday morning.

Mother died of a stroke at the age of sixty-eight and father, who married Angela some five years later, died of respiratory complications at eighty-six. They both worked hard and played hard – a gene luckily passed down to both my brother and me.

CHAPTER 2

EDUCATING EMSON

When I was five, I attended Brunswick House School in Maidstone, a primary school with a good reputation that was a ten-minute bus ride from my home.

From day one I seemed to struggle with school, where the teachers were, on the whole, middle-aged women. The headmistress, Phyllis Foster, a formidable character with rather too many lipstick-smudged teeth, spoke with a large plum in her mouth and always referred to me as Clive EmOWson. Perhaps she just couldn't get the words out phonetically. However, it did prepare me for a life of my name being mis-pronounced such as Emerson. Emberson. Empson, Clive Anderson to name but a few.

Mrs Foster made it abundantly clear to my parents that as I was dyslexic, I would have no hope of passing the 11+, so they decided to send me to King's Junior School to increase my chances of passing the common entrance exam to join the senior school at thirteen. The logic nearly worked. Three of us failed, one was asked to leave, one had to stay on in the junior school for another year and I was invited to join the fourth form on report – not a good start.

To be a success at public school in the late 1950s one had to be either academic, sporty, compliant or, in some cases, physically attractive. Sadly, I possessed none of these qualities. Consequently, my five years at King's Rochester had to be tolerated by all parties on a daily basis.

Academically I was labelled an FLB – Fat Lazy Bastard – or, in today's more enlightened terms, I was dyslexic. Team sport was not my thing either – why run three miles when there is a bus on the same route? – and rugby was a particular nightmare. By the time I had waddled from one scrum to the next line up on the other side of the field it was time to get into another scrum. I loved cricket, it was nice and gentle and one was personally responsible when either batting or bowling. However, to get a reasonable game, you had to be liked by the games teacher. Oh well!

Many successful entrepreneurs are noted for a poor school career and it is not difficult to understand the reason why. For those who do precisely what they are told, as and when instructed to do so and without question, school can be an easy ride. However, to question why is not appreciated nor is using one's initiative encouraged, while answering back can be quite painful in every respect.

I did enjoy Scouts, but being a troublemaker in class sadly did not make promotion to patrol leader an option. The worst day of the week for me was Thursday – Combined Cadet Force (CCF) day. My humour was one of my main downfalls in the early days; used as a defence mechanism but stupidly directed to the prefects, NCOs and masters. Apparently, the answer to 'I didn't see you at the camouflage exercise this morning, Emson' is not 'Thank you very much, Sarge.'

I misunderstood the meaning of using one's initiative too. Once we were all put on a coach and driven over the River

Medway then told to use our initiative to get back to school. There would of course be guards on the bridge. While the others were getting into teams, I wandered back and hid on the coach, which duly took me and the officers back again. Apparently, that is not using one's initiative, but I still don't understand why. I reasoned that guards should also have been put on the bus too, a basic error they found difficult to accept.

So, at the age of sixteen it was decided that I would be better off without school and they would certainly be better off without me. I was not expelled but, as I have found ever since, timing is everything!

I was, however, proud of the school and remained a paid-up member of the Old Roffensian Society. To my surprise, in 2006 I received a call asking if I would become its President. I suggested a check be made that they had the right person, as I had left at sixteen, to the relief of all concerned.

'Oh no,' came the reply. 'We know who you are and thought it might encourage the present-day failures that there is life beyond school.'

I took it as a compliment. Not a lot changes.

Sue and I were invited to dinner with the headmaster and the committee but, sad to say, I put the wrong date in my newly-introduced electronic diary. Imagine the embarrassment when Sue took the call on Saturday morning asking where we were the previous night. She insisted that the dinner was the following Friday and even confirmed that we had booked a driver for the evening. The mistake cost me a dinner for twelve in one of the best restaurants in Kent as an apology.

The President takes office at the annual dinner but, having not been back to the school since I'd left, I was unaware of the protocol. As we sat down the secretary asked if I had nominated anyone to say grace, so I immediately turned to the headmaster to ask if he would do the honours. It all came flooding back when he pondered over whether to do it in Latin, Greek or English.

'It's your gig,' said I. 'Whichever you feel most comfortable with.'

I might have guessed the answer would be that he was of course 'comfortable' with all three. He did it in Latin, I congratulated him on doing it in Greek and so started three years of banter as we each vied for the high ground.

I thoroughly enjoyed my three-year term as President and was advised that it was an interesting, if different, experience from my predecessors. One of the most moving duties was the laying of the Old Roffensian wreath in the cathedral on Commemoration Day, together with those from the school, to remember the brave young men who had perished in the theatres of war, and whose names were read out during the service.

After we laid our wreaths, we stood to one side as the students lined up to remove the poppy from their lapel and place it on the plinth. As one pupil of oriental origin shuffled forward with a bored look and hands in his pockets, I shouted 'Take your hands out of your pockets, lad.' He stood to attention and looked up as if the voice had emanated from God.

'We don't talk to the boys like that anymore,' came the immediate response from the headmaster, to which I replied, 'And doesn't it show, headmaster.' As always, the pendulum swings too far the other way.

My first Old Roffensian Dinner as president was held in Leeds Castle, near Maidstone. I was sitting next to the Dean of Rochester, Adrian Newman, and remarked that it was a pity the event was not held in Rochester. He said the reason was that there wasn't a big enough building, to which I pointed out that the cathedral was both a massive and beautiful building, so why not hold it in the nave – a stunning setting and a fitting location?

Apparently, the floor is Grade I-listed and could be damaged, but the following year, after much discussion and persuasion, the dinner was held in the crypt for the very first time. It was a sell-out and the start of many more fundraising dinners for the cathedral. I used the team I knew and trusted from the charity fundraising events Sue and I had been hosting at home for years to provide the tables, chairs, cutlery, crockery and catering.

Some ten years after the seed was sown, and following many more dinners in the crypt, a successful fundraising banquet was eventually held in the nave for more than 200 and attended by the patron of Rochester Cathedral, HRH Sophie Wessex.

I have enjoyed regular visits to the school since handing over the reins and the experience has taught me, if nothing else, that my less-than-sparkling performance during my time at King's was not entirely their fault.

However, I have no doubt that without the grounding King's Rochester gave me in the way of respect, discipline and the ability to communicate with my peers, my life would have taken a significantly different path. I wish, also, that I had appreciated just what sacrifices my parents made to send me there, but sadly, that seldom occurs in one's formative teenage years. They never showed just how frustrated and disappointed they must have felt about my lack of performance. Hopefully I have made up for it in later years, but that I will never know as they were not around when I eventually found success.

Apparently, potential O-levels in English and divinity are not enough to enter any chosen profession (apart from Estate Agency perhaps where I could write the details and then pray I would sell the property) and it was therefore decided that a few more qualifications would be advantageous, so I applied to attend Maidstone Technical College.

At the interview I told the panel that I really wanted to study law and I was duly moved to the commerce course, where we studied accounts and bookkeeping, economics, economic history, commerce, English and mathematics. These were all subjects that appealed to me and I could see a purpose in studying them as they would be useful in the real world.

Frankly, I couldn't care less how many wives Henry VIII had, but I was intrigued by the Industrial Revolution, the South Sea Bubble in 1720 and other periods in economic history which continue to repeat themselves. For example, we are now reversing the move from the countryside to the towns that took place from the mid-1750s, with businesses now relocating back into rural enterprise centres. Lower rates, free parking, fewer traffic delays.

I also liked the fact that there were no rules – if you didn't attend or work, that was your decision. We had to dress smartly, but there was no uniform as such. Finally, I was being treated as an adult and with nothing to fight against, I concentrated on learning the subjects that stimulated me.

The atmosphere appealed to me too. My fellow students came from all walks of life and we were treated with some respect. I learned to be socially mobile, mixing with a few other failed public school boys but mainly students from secondary modern schools. It was at Maidstone Technical College that I met Mike King-Lewis, the son of a brigadier. He had also struggled at boarding school but in time Mike would change my life.

My two years at the college gave me not only five O-levels and an A-level in accounts and bookkeeping, thanks to the patience of Tom Reid-Marr and John Parr, but also showed me that if you enjoy what you are doing, success is likely to follow. I certainly respond more to encouragement than criticism, as do many of the young people I mentor.

During my college holidays I worked as a bus conductor for Maidstone Corporation, another environment where concealing a privileged lifestyle was essential to enjoying a happy working relationship with colleagues. I think that's where I honed the chameleon-like qualities which have stood me in good stead all my life. I can talk to lords and travellers alike, the only difference being that when a traveller shakes your hand, he means it, whereas the aristocracy tend to renege on the deal once they've consulted their financial advisers, family and friends!

It was working on the buses that introduced me to the unions for the first time; apparently, I was volunteering for all the less-attractive shifts, which commanded a higher hourly pay. The shed crew was the worst; I had to be at the depot at 5.30am to cover in case of illness. Quite often I would sit around for three hours before being released to go home. The other unpopular one was a straight eight-hour late turn on Sundays. The union rep approached me to say that I was taking away quality earning time from his members just because I wasn't paying tax. Naturally, I agreed to stand down, only to learn that the next Sunday night bus had to be cancelled as there was no crew to staff it.

It certainly proved a lucrative interlude between college terms before finding a proper job.

CHAPTER 3

SO TO WORK

Having left college, it was time to get a proper job – the career prospects on the buses did not seem too attractive. I really wanted to study law but without Latin that would prove difficult. After five years studying the subject at school, the only phrase I could remember was 'Caesar amore mensae' which means 'Caesar made love to the table.' We even named one of our dogs Caesar, but instead of the table he had other interests and I didn't know the Latin for 'screwing the scrawny mongrel from next door,' so in the sixty years since I left school, I have not had an opportunity to impress my educated friends with my prowess in Latin.

I wanted a job where I wasn't tied to the office from 9am to 5.30pm, so banking and accountancy were not an option. My brother seemed to enjoy being in estate agency, which for me had most of the elements I was looking for: each day different with a variety of properties to see and the all-important meeting people and thrill of selling. Plus, of course, getting out in the car for viewings and inspections. I had a passion for cars from an early age and the prospect of driving around the county and being paid to do so really appealed.

My first job was with Geering & Colyer in Earl Street, Maidstone under the supervision of John Yeandle, who had moved with his wife and small son from the West Country to open the new branch. His number two was Don Cook, the surveyor and office manager.

John had a Hillman Minx, which I blew up on the M2 and Don had a Mini, which I thrashed round Kent like a rally driver. I must have been a real thorn in their sides and they moved me on as soon as they possibly could. An opportunity presented itself when my brother persuaded his employer, WER Randall & Sons in Medway, to buy the first firm he worked for, Hillier French & Son in Maidstone – just four doors up from Geering & Colyer.

'Potential conflict of interest' was the reason they gave and so off I went to Chatham as an articled clerk to one Charles Arthur Dawson Cole, a chartered surveyor with WER Randall & Sons ,who devoted most of his day to building society surveys, or valuations as they are called today.

I think that the eighteen months I spent at Chatham was probably the lowest point of my career. I was on £3.50 a week, running a clapped-out motor scooter, doing a mundane job holding the end of a tape for a boss who clearly had more interest in golf on a Saturday morning than inspecting boxes in the back streets of the Medway Towns. The real business was conducted by senior partner Claude Harris, a brilliant man whose estuary accent went down well with the wheelers and dealers in the Medway Towns at that time.

In those days there were only five or six estate agents, of which the two largest were WER Randall and their main rival JD Walter and Sons, with whom they subsequently merged. It gave me enormous pleasure when we acquired the property auction division of Walter & Randall – albeit a lifetime later.

My next move was, like so many others, totally unexpected and down to pure fate. A good friend from my tech college days, Mike King-Lewis, was working for Ibbett Mosley Card & Co in Tunbridge Wells and saw what he thought was his own job advertised. He asked if I could apply for it to see if it was actually his job, because if he did so it would show that he was looking to move.

In fact, the position was for a junior negotiator in the recently opened Tonbridge branch under the managership of Charles Kinloch, a young chartered surveyor. I went for the interview and impressed Charles with my A-level in accounts and bookkeeping, as he found the accounts side of the rent collection part of the business challenging.

So, out of the blue, I was elevated to junior negotiator on £10 a week plus commission. Enough to buy a Riley 1.5 followed by a Mini, which I managed to trash in no time at all. Indeed, I wasn't able to sell a car until I was twenty-six, as I destroyed them one by one in trees, ditches and hedgerows and the insurance companies were kind enough to reimburse me for the wrecks that I left scattered around the county.

My time at Ibbett Mosely Card & Co in Tonbridge gave me as much enjoyment as any part of my career. We were a small team and individual performances made a real difference. Charles was a great bloke to work for while the firm's senior partner, Humphrey Wickham, was a man I admired and feared in equal proportions. On a regular basis he would come down to Tonbridge and invite me to join him for lunch at Gunners, the local department store, on the basis that he would pay for the meal and I would leave the sixpence tip. The only problem was that in those days I never had any money by Wednesday, so very often Charles would slip me the coin as we were leaving the office.

The highlight of his visit was that on occasion he asked me to drive him back to Sevenoaks in his Vanden Plas Princess R, a luxury saloon in sage green, powered by a three-litre Rolls-Royce engine. Such luxury and a real treat.

We were a good team but it had to come to an end when I met Charles' sister, Sue. A girlfriend stood me up at short notice one Saturday night (yes, I was surprised too!) and Charles announced that his sister was down from London that weekend and she wasn't that fussy, so would probably come out with me.

Sue and I hit it off immediately, despite being two totally different people – she was from London and I was still living at home in Maidstone – and within eighteen months we were engaged to be married.

As we grew closer together, we both realised, of course, that working for her brother was not ideal and that a move was inevitable. I saw an advertisement in the *Estates Gazette* for junior partner designate in a general practice in Dorset, a county we both love. The sole principal was looking to retire in five years. The interview went well, but during our conversation he mentioned that his son was studying at the college of estate management. Although offered the position I declined; it was not quite what I had envisaged from the advert – one of the downsides of being an eternal optimist.

At about this time I bumped into John Heddle at a charity boxing match in Maidstone. He was a young, larger-than-life character and, to this day, the best auctioneer I have ever seen. His personality simply oozed zest and enthusiasm and he always had a ready smile and the most amazing memory for names and jokes. He was a wit and raconteur and used his skill to full advantage from the rostrum. After meeting him you always left feeling far happier than when you arrived.

John mentioned that he wanted a young ambassador for his practice in Folkestone and asked me to join him and his senior partner, Colonel NC Butler (Winky to his friends) at a generous £20 a week. A more diverse match you couldn't find. The Colonel was an upright, long-established member of Hythe society (his original telephone number was Hythe 2), chairman of the bench and trustee to numerous charities. John, at thirty years his junior, was seen by many as brash and forward, but he was a good businessman and used Winky's contacts to build up an amazing practice. I got on really well with the Colonel, helped I think by the fact that he was also an Old Roffensian and this was an era when the old school tie was not something to be ashamed of.

Not long after I joined Heddle Butler, they bought Winky's old firm FW Butler & Co in Hythe and asked me to manage the new business. I was twenty-four years old and it was my first introduction to the world of auctioneering.

Butlers had a chattels saleroom – far from fine art, more a collection of what the trade called suppository furniture – the sort of thing you take home and put up yourself. In the 1970s the general rule was that the senior partner conducted the auctions, whether he was capable or not. John and Winky, however, held a more modern view; if a person is up to the task, let them do it. How fortunate was I to benefit from such an ethos.

My introduction to the rostrum, however, came a little quicker than even I had anticipated. One wet Wednesday morning the Colonel came to work with gout, following a poor night's sleep. It was a general sale, I was clerking when, without warning, one of the dealers made a cheeky bid and the Colonel declared that he was too old to put up with this nonsense and that I should take the rostrum and finish the sale.

Finish? It had only just begun.

'Who is to do the clerking?' I protested, to which came the reply, 'You sort it out, laddie' as he stomped back to his office. My initiation into auctioneering had begun. Fortunately, the audience at that sale saw the situation and was extremely kind and tolerant. Before the next auction I ventured to suggest to Winky that perhaps I could conduct the sale from the beginning and thus be able to organise a clerk in advance. 'Whatever' came the reply. I was elated at the opportunity denied by so many of my contemporaries, until the auction actually began. It soon became clear that the last sale was the honeymoon period; now it was gloves off and them against me.

I was really happy at Heddle Butler in Hythe, bringing them from a loss to the leading estate agent in the town, modernising the practice where possible, despite protestations from the established staff. The deal I had with John Heddle was that once the Hythe branch was in profit I would be offered a partnership – age still being no barrier.

However, little did I realise that John had far loftier ambitions than just being an estate agent in Folkestone and Hythe. He wanted the London life and to become a Member of Parliament, a position he eventually achieved. In the interim he brought in a chartered surveyor to run the practice. This chap mentioned during an early visit to Hythe that if I kept my nose clean and qualified as a chartered surveyor, after ten years I might be considered worthy of joining the partnership. When I told him that the deal with John was that when the branch was in profit, the partnership would be offered to me, I was told that John had moved on and 'Let's face it, you've just got married, you've got a three-month-old baby and a mortgage – you won't be going anywhere.' A lesson in man management that has served me well ever since.

Within three months of that exchange and with John's blessing, he introduced me to Neil Alexander at the Cheriton branch of the National Westminster Bank and arranged an unsecured overdraft of £2,500 (the equivalent of £25,000 today). I used it to open my first estate agency at 16 High Street, Hythe. Over the next ten years I opened branches in Dymchurch, New Romney, Lydd and Sellindge, as well as an auction room at the Old Post Office in Hythe.

It was hard work and far from plain sailing, as when I opened the door, I was the seventh estate agent in a relatively small seaside town. I needed to differentiate my practice from the others. I persuaded my brother to hold a copy of my register in his Mayfair office so that the advertisements stated 'also at London W1.' Not only was I the London agent but also the first to open on a Saturday afternoon and at lunchtimes.

I ran the office with a junior negotiator, one full-time and one part-time secretary. I collected the rents on Sunday mornings and quite often managed show houses for a couple of hours on Sunday afternoons. In some evenings before an auction I would arrange the lots with the junior negotiator. Clearly, none of this would have been possible without the total support and understanding from Sue, who was left to look after the children while I was out, apart from one night a week, when she would pop down to clean the office while I babysat Becky and James, who was just a few months old. Once a month Sue would clerk at the Saturday auctions, Father would look after the accounts and Mother would look after the children. A total family affair.

However, after ten years spent running my own business and auction room in the Romney Marsh region, I was becoming frustrated at not being able to expand in areas that were not dominated by Ward and Partners. They had already got a stronghold in Ashford and I'd also I had heard on the grapevine that they were looking to open in Folkestone too – thus effectively surrounding me.

Ward and Partners were a formidable force to take on, brilliantly run by a small partnership of five and way ahead of the competition. They produced a newspaper called *Property Mail,* which was delivered free to every household in their operational area, their offices were bright and their staff well-trained. Senior partner Dennis Paulley had been instrumental in creating one of the first and certainly the most successful collective multi-lot property auctions in Kent.

It was definitely time to make a phone call.

CHAPTER 4

FROM SOLE PROPRIETOR TO CORPORATE COMPANY

I phoned one of the directors at Ward & Partners with whom I'd been at school to ask whether a merger might be considered. His view was that Hythe was a long way from the Medway Towns and would mean using a lot of petrol – as droll as ever! However, within a week I heard from Graham Smith, one of the two managing partners, who said that I'd spoken to the wrong person and would I like lunch?

He brought with him Tony Smith (no relation) to see my offices and have a chat. Dennis Paulley appeared at my next furniture sale and, unbeknown to me at the time, decided that he'd found the right person to take over the auction department as and when he retired.

The deal was done. I was now an associate partner in the largest and most successful estate agency business in the county, paid more than I had been earning on my own and now with the whole of Kent in which to spread my ever-ambitious wings.

The next three years with Ward & Partners were very special indeed. Graham and Tony had the perfect ethos for success: invest in the business. Their thinking was that if you have the best person in a secondary location, you have half a chance of succeeding and if you have the prime location but a mediocre person in place, you have also half a chance at succeeding. However, put the best person in a prime location, then success is inevitable. There were occasions when a prime site would be mothballed waiting for the right person and at other times a good person would be employed in an existing branch waiting for the right premises to be acquired.

My auction room was being fed from all nine branches (fourteen after my acquisition), which improved the quality and released me to do other things once a manager had been appointed to run the saleroom. The management and survey departments were centralised to Medway, leaving my branches to concentrate solely on house sales and mortgages. As predicted, within months Wards opened in Folkestone and I appointed Yvonne, the best salesperson I have ever worked with, while I was moved to the new branch as the local partner.

Yvonne was amazing at her job – she swore like a trooper and chain-smoked, yet always looked immaculate in her designer clothes and could sell an igloo to an Eskimo. Folkestone was in the top five offices for sales within months of opening. We actually took over the established firm Milne Sherwood and completely gutted and renovated the building which was, of course, in the best position in town.

The *modus operandi* was simple; each partner had their own responsibility and managed their role individually. Tony managed the fleet of cars, Graham the mailing system and promotion of the company, Dennis was the figurehead, property auctioneer and ambassador, I looked after premises and equipment. If anyone complained about their allocation of a car, for example, it was handled by Tony; if they wanted a new photocopier then I sorted it.

The mailing under Graham was a bit of a confetti approach. Too many times a buyer would insist on a bungalow and a garage and end up buying a three-bedroom house with just an off-road parking space. How frustrating when you also had that property on the books but didn't send it to them because it wasn't what they wanted! Sending everything to everyone solved the problem. We would, of course, get the odd complaint that we were wasting our time sending unwanted circulars, but we pointed out that it was our money and if they didn't like it, bin it. The sales proved that the system worked.

Within three years of my joining Wards, the business expanded from fourteen to thirty-four branches, all well-managed and maintained. Now the undisputed leading brand in Kent, it was a vibrant, exciting time where every day was different and rewarding. During that period Lloyds Bank ventured into estate agency by taking over Geering & Colyer and other leading brands around the country.

Then, in 1986, estate agency offices became a breeding ground for institutions to buy up successful businesses as a way of selling their core brands. Ward & Partners were clearly a prime target and were approached by Prudential Property Services, a subsidiary of the giant insurance company and to whom the many millions spent on developing the new business were mere peanuts in the overall picture.

The price they paid for Ward & Partners was eyewatering and Dennis Paulley made it clear that he would retire on the day of completion once the deal was done. I was in the right place at the right time for a change, and became auctioneer for the company.

And thus a new era began. The logic behind the Prudential way of thinking was to buy the eight most successful businesses around the UK, whatever the cost, then sell their insurance and mortgage products through their own branch network. Up until then, the image of the 'man from the Pru' was of a chap in bicycle clips working out of a third-floor backstreet office and collecting small premiums from house to house. Overnight, they had a high street presence in virtually every town in the UK.

What the powers that be had not envisaged was firstly, the eight core businesses were each run by proven entrepreneurs with complete knowledge of the business and their own ideas about how to continue to run their successful offices. Secondly, the mortgage and property insurance products offered by Prudential were uncompetitive in the marketplace. Not something that sits easily with a corporate body, whose answer was to bring in somebody with no knowledge or experience in the profession and give him free rein to reinvent the wheel – even if his version of the wheel was that it should be square.

Right on cue, enter a certain Mr Bradley with the apt initials of JCB – known for their capacity to destruct on demand. A short little man with a misplaced sense of his own ability, he came from a background alien to the estate agency business and his method was to get rid of anyone who knew what they were talking about and replace them with a panel of 'yes men.' Needless to say, meetings were somewhat fraught when JCB arrived at 9am on a Monday morning in his chauffeur-driven Jaguar to announce more closures and a list of which valuable and loyal members of staff were to be made redundant.

This type of approach was not limited to just Prudential Property Services, as with any organisation, whether Government, business or institution, it is not a good career move for the number two to tell the person at the top he is wrong and so the boss subsequently gains a false impression of his or her own ability.

Sadly, lessons are never learned, as witnessed some thirty years later when Joe's modern equivalent, Allison Platt, single-handedly destroyed the Countrywide estate agency business within three years, during which time the shares fell from around £10 to less than 10p. And what I find appalling is that the board congratulated itself when they got rid of her but took absolutely no action or responsibility during the period of destruction.

Luckily, my remit at the Prudential was to take charge of all departments in our region from Essex to the Isle of Wight, with the exception of house sales and financial services. I appointed a head of each division covering property and fine art auctions, surveys, management, lettings, commercial, land and new homes. I was a director on the regional board and also national property auctioneer for all the regions and continued to work with Graham Smith on acquisitions. The salary was massive for the time, but clearly unsustainable.

The first year with PPS was enjoyable. For the first time, I witnessed for myself just how easy it is to spend other people's money, which appeared to come from a bottomless pit. Losses on the sales side were mounting as ill-conceived changes in strategy went unchallenged.

For instance, at Ward & Partners we paid the branch manager a small salary supplemented by 10 per cent of the gross takings of the branch. In Ashford the manager was on £50,000 a year from the £500,000 turnover he created, our view being that he took £50,000 and we managed on the other £450,000 to run the business.

The thought police in London, however, decided that £50,000 was far too much for a mere salesman and that the figure could become even greater if sales increased as predicted. Their answer was to pay a basic salary calculated at 90 per cent of the average earnings over the previous three years, plus a small commission. Little did anyone foresee the property collapse of 1988/9 where sales plummeted and turnover dropped by 50 per cent or more. So now the manager was on £45,000 against a turnover of

£200,000 – and obviously going nowhere, however badly he was treated!

One of the problems with over-expansion was buying incompatible businesses to get the desired national coverage of 1,000 branches. It was difficult managing staff who had taken the golden egg but wanted nothing to change -–the same mentality seen in expecting a free lunch; there's no such thing!

One of my greatest challenges was David, who ran the Sevenoaks fine art department, a former partner of the highly-respected Parsons, Welch & Cowell. He despised everything about the 'vulgar' Prudential – their colours, ethos, management and, most of all, me, the devil employed to impose on him the required standards of the fine art division. The only thing he did like was the inordinate amount of money paid for the practice.

When I first met him following the takeover, we talked about the computerised Prudential fine art accounting package (which he said was not needed as his wife did it all by hand). At my first visit I asked him how he handled cataloguing mistakes, which were inevitable when compiling 800 to 1,000 lots on a regular basis. I was informed that he had never made a mistake in his life, so he was somewhat taken aback when I told him that he had just made the biggest mistake in his life in treating me like an idiot and that he would find out the error of his ways in no time.

Indeed, about six months later I received a call from David's assistant who explained that he did not wish to be disloyal to his line manager, but was in an invidious position as a painting which David had attributed to a particular artist was disputed by both Sotheby's and Christie's. He told me that if he kept quiet and the error came to light, he would be implicated in the cover up. I told him not to worry – I appreciated the call, but as far as I was concerned the conversation never took place.

A few days later I popped into the Sevenoaks saleroom 'while passing' and told David that I had heard that there was a problem over a painting. The seller wanted his £3,500 and the buyer wanted a refund despite David insisting that the London experts were wrong. Such an arrogant little man. I did not reveal my source but reminded him that I knew most of the buyers and sellers and that word soon spreads. This is just the type of story that could make headlines in the local press, so I told David to give the buyer his money back, pay the seller and give me the painting.

I offered the picture a few months later in the Hythe sale room described merely as 'Cows drinking from a pond.' There were a couple of buyers who thought that I had missed the significance of the artist and the painting sold for £3,700. As I had not alluded to any particular artist there was, of course, no comeback.

Although it might seem like a relatively minor point, all members of staff were required to wear a company tie while on duty. Predictably, I was told by David that he had managed to dress himself since he was eight years old and wouldn't be changing that now. Oh dear. Within two weeks his lovely BMW was replaced with a sign-written Ford Sierra from the sales fleet. His wife was horrified but I pointed out that the car was not for his wife but for business and if it was that embarrassing, to leave it in the car park overnight. After a week or so catching the bus in to work, he decided that a tie was preferable to keeping a 'cigarette salesman's car' parked in his exclusive road. What a lot of nonsense, but nonetheless an issue that had to be addressed. The BMW was duly returned.

The fine art side of the business never really sat well with London, as it was incapable of fitting the management information into the neat little boxes loved by accountants. As always, give an accountant a problem and he will devise a box with which to solve it. Furthermore, auctions are high profile and very public if things go wrong; they were not adding to the core part of the business and, frankly, JCB just did not understand them.

I received a memo from London asking for the number of employees in the fine art salerooms and their length of service, which is basic information required when a sale is being considered. I mentioned in a fax that if they were thinking of selling off that division, the lease at Rye prevented the sales office (which had just been the subject of an £80,000 refurbishment) being split from the auction room that lay behind.

This was a deliberate act by Colin Stutely (a former partner of Vidler and Co, whom we had bought) to ensure the continuance of the business. I was told to just do as I was told and London would sort out any 'minor parochial problems.' After the business was hived off to Phillips, the sales office remained closed for eight years until Colin took it back again, having enjoyed the rent for the preceding period. An application to the court for a variation of the terms of the lease was rejected by the judge who found no grounds for such an application. So much for sorting out minor parochial problems.

Suffice it to say, I only learned from the *Antiques Trade Gazette* that three auction rooms over which I was regional director had been sold in a national deal. The phone calls from concerned employees wanting information were streaming in, but with no real answers to give them. The personal hardship and consequences to the people on whom such decisions were made were of no importance. Cannon fodder at worst.

A side issue to the story is that I dashed down to Rye to see the long-standing employees whom we had inherited from Vidler & Co., only to find that I had jumped the red lights at a rail crossing on the Rye to Romney Road. I had no recollection of the event, even when the British Transport policeman called at my home some days later to discuss the matter.

'Why didn't you stop me at the time?' I asked.

'We weren't there but you were reported by the signal box operator.'

'So, it's his word against mine then,' I argued.

'The signal box operators don't make mistakes,' I was told, to which I replied that I was not sure the casualties in the Clapham Common train crash would agree. At this remark, he put on his bobby's pointed hat and stood up, banging his head on the low beams in our sitting room. The fine was £60, but no points on my licence.

The Hythe saleroom was closed immediately, making Sue redundant by fax. Rye followed a couple of years later. Sevenoaks, however, thrived under the new regime and I did not miss having to manage David any longer. He was not happy with his new employer. There was a saying at the time that Sotheby's were gentlemen trying to be auctioneers, while Christie's were auctioneers trying to be gentlemen and Philips were neither. Fair or not, I will leave you to decide.

The three years at the Pru were interesting and yet frustrating. Having to implement ridiculous policies and losing excellent staff was extremely unpleasant. The first year was exciting as all new systems were being introduced. The magic money tree was loaded with fruit. I was out of the firing line, as long as my divisions made money I was left alone – the main focus was clearly on house sales and mortgages.

I enjoyed working with Graham on the many acquisitions, despite knowing that the synergy of some of the businesses we bought would cause problems. We took over some brilliant practices along the south coast but, sadly, demotivated them and destroyed them, usually within months.

In the second year it became clear that the model was unsustainable and by the third year, for the first time in my career, I hated going to work. I knew it was time to move on and precipitated the decision when in a board meeting JCB used the ridiculous and meaningless phrase 'I hear what you say.' The response, out of lack of respect and utter contempt was 'I am not suggesting you are deaf, Mr Bradley, just dim on this part of the business as well.'

He came into my office after the meeting and said there wasn't room for both of us in the business – I agreed and asked him rather cheekily where he was going, to which the reply was 'You don't understand, do you?'

I was ready with my plans for the next venture but, unexpectedly, made to work my full three months' notice.

CHAPTER 5

MEET SUE

Sue was welcomed with open arms when she joined the Emson family in February 1971.

We had met two years earlier when I was working for her brother in Tonbridge. At the time she was living in London and working as a secretary, but not long after we were introduced, she moved to Kent and took a flat in Tunbridge Wells, initially working for a local accountant. A later career change saw her moving in and looking after families where the mother was recovering from an illness and Sue would take over the running of the house and children.

She worked in this capacity for two families, one of which has remained close friends. Erica has always treated Sue as a member of the family because, without her, their second son, David, would not have been born.

When we first met neither of us had any intention or thought of getting married. Sue had a bad experience when her parents broke up and found it difficult to trust anybody long term. I was only twenty-three, far too young and anyway, Sue was a massive two years my senior!

Despite the reservations, it was a whirlwind romance – I was living in Maidstone, working in Folkestone and seeing Sue in Tunbridge Wells two or three times a week and at weekends.

In August 1970 she went to the Dordogne for a two-week holiday with her stepmother Judy and the four children and I went with farmer Chris and seven other friends to the South of France with the ski boat.

We both missed each other very much and, on our return, I asked Sue to marry me. Her response was, 'Can I keep my car?' which really meant 'Oh yes, I thought you'd never ask!' It was, without doubt, the best decision of our lives. During the six months of our engagement, Sue moved into London Road and was the daughter my mother and father never had. They doted on her and she felt truly loved.

Our honeymoon was spent in Mevagissey but the trip to Cornwall was somewhat tiring as the week before the wedding I blew up the engine on my Triumph 2000, so we had to do the long journey in her Mini Countryman.

On our return from honeymoon, we moved into our newly refurbished house in Sellindge. Life, we thought, could not be better. How wrong we were; exactly nine months to the day after our wedding, Rebecca Jane was born. When Sue first became pregnant many of my friends questioned whether I had jumped the gun and I made a few bob from some side bets when our daughter appeared, on time, on 5 November 1971.

We had planned on having four children but, sadly, it was not to be. Sue suffered two miscarriages between Becky's birth and James' arrival. Naturally, we were both absolutely distraught and Sue blamed herself which, although apparently a normal reaction, was completely inexplicable. When the original miscarriage happened, it was extremely emotional for both of us and the first time Sue had seen me cry. The second and only other time was when the reality suddenly hit me, standing in the Southampton Hospital car park, that my mother was going to die.

Our gynaecologist, Kenneth Poole, advised after the second miscarriage that Sue would have to stay in bed for seven months if she was to have any hope of carrying a baby for the full term. Mrs Fuller, a farmer's wife from Sellindge who had been Becky's babysitter, agreed to help out. I would get Becky up and take her with me to collect Brenda each weekday morning at 8am, then head off to open the office at 9am. At 6pm after work I then drove Brenda back home and looked after Sue and Becky.

My parents would arrive on Friday evening to take Becky home for the weekend, returning her on Sunday night. Mrs Fuller's cooking, and especially the daily fry-up of delicious doughnuts, was not good for my figure and Becky was over-indulged every weekend by my doting parents. However, it was a small price to pay, the plan worked and James Robert was born on 20 June 1974.

Sue set the temperature in the house, was a brilliant mother and wife and produced two children of whom we have always been immensely proud. She should take the credit for their lovely nature and success; the family and home were her domain, which she managed without fault or complaint.

A successful marriage is as much about luck as judgement, but I put our happiness down to the fact that we were neither critical nor judgemental and only ever had eyes for each other, thereby enjoying total trust. We never argued over money and, indeed, when we went through the 'famine' of 1989-1992, I didn't realise until later that for three years Sue didn't buy herself any new clothes whatsoever. The little money available went on the children. We enjoyed mutual respect and, I believe, both felt that we were punching above our weight.

In 2007 we discovered, in the space of a single day, that Sue had breast cancer and also needed open-heart surgery to replace her aortic valve. We were in shock at the news and our local GP, Dr Koria, came round immediately to talk us through the procedure. He said it would be up to the surgeons to decide which operation took precedence.

The chemotherapy on the breast worked, as did the valve replacement at a private hospital in London. Sue took the whole thing in her stride.

We had planned on spending three weeks in the villa after the heart operation for her to convalesce. We were told that it would be OK to fly as lots of patients came to the UK for the procedure. However, a slight complication meant that the drugs Sue needed to take prevented flying or exposure to sunlight for a fortnight. She still wanted to go, so we drove down. Marriage was never meant to be twenty-one hours in a car together; I wanted to go one way, Sue another and Satnav a different route altogether.

Sue was also extremely uncomfortable and had a pillow under her seat belt to soften the pressure from the surgery on her breast bone. If I drove too fast it hurt her as we went round corners and braked and if I went too slowly, we would have to stay another night en route – the epitome of a no-win situation. The relaxation at the villa was worth the effort, however, and I arranged for our handyman Charlie to fly down and take the car back while Sue and I picked up his car which he had left at Gatwick.

Sue made a complete recovery but within three years there was more bad news. Following stomach cramps, she was diagnosed with bowel cancer. More chemotherapy, a six-hour operation with two surgeons as the growth had attached itself to her ovary and bowel. As always, Sue faced the hazard with amazing bravery, a positive attitude and good humour, which were all vital elements towards a successful outcome.

She was extremely weak after the procedure and I stayed with her most of the time. Her blood pressure was low and she was prone to fainting, especially if she rushed downstairs to answer the door. I did receive a couple of phone calls from delivery men to say that Sue had collapsed in the hall, but I was never more than thirty minutes away.

I took her to the hairdresser in Hythe on one occasion and waited outside. One of the girls came out and said that Sue had fainted and they'd called an ambulance. I told her to ring back and cancel it and that after a glass of water and a sit-down, she would be fine. When she had recovered enough, I walked her to the car and then returned to the shop to pay the bill. No wonder she fainted!

When Sue passed away in March 2020, following a complication with her aortic valve, I spread all the photographs of our privileged life together across the snooker table and realised just how fortunate I had been to spend most of my life with such a super person. I am grateful that she went first, as I would not have wanted her to suffer the inevitable loss that the survivor of a loyal union endures.

I have enjoyed the support and comfort of Rebecca and James, their four very special children and so many close friends too numerous to mention. Rebecca married Steve in 1998 and a more loyal, lovely son-in-law it would be impossible to imagine; their children Alex and Livvy are a tribute to them both.

James married Kate in 2001. Kate sadly died of cancer in 2016 at just forty-one, leaving Tom and Charlie, then aged fourteen and nine. She was much loved, as witnessed by the 300 mourners at her funeral. James is now with Rachel who clearly cherishes every moment with him and gives him the love and support he so richly deserves.

It is, of course, impossible to condense fifty years together within a few short paragraphs, but my feelings were probably best described in the following tribute I paid to Sue at her funeral, conducted by our dear friend Canon

Norman Woods and attended by just ten family members under the strict Covid rules at the time.

'I wanted to pay this tribute to Sue for two reasons. Firstly, apart from her brother Charles and stepmother Judy, I have probably known Sue for longer than anyone else and, having been together for fifty years, I certainly know her better than anyone else.

Sue would have been very happy that the service was just for the immediate family; it is what she wanted for her seventy-fifthth birthday last year and what she would have wanted today.

'She loved nothing more than when Becky and James and later the grandchildren and their friends dropped into Bitford for a chat, for birthday parties or just to sit on the sofa and chill. It always brought that lovely smile to her face. She was easy to be with, non-confrontational, non-judgemental, always ready to listen and give her opinion if asked. And also appreciative of the old jokes, however many times she had heard them.

'We are only a small gathering here today, but I can assure you that there are hundreds joining us in spirit if not in body. Sue was well loved and respected by so many, especially her small coterie of really close friends.

'We were privileged to have Sue in our lives as a mother, grandmother, wife, sister and friend. She didn't have an evil bone in her body or nasty thought in her head and was never one for material things, regarding people as far more important than possessions, especially when in small gatherings.

'She would not have wanted to go so soon and miss seeing her beloved grandchildren achieve their varied aims in life and she would have been very sad that Alex was unable to be with us today. However, she was very proud of you all and would have appreciated the parts that each of you have played in today's service and indeed, her life.

'You all saw how loyal and patient Sue was as a wife; she tolerated me very well and without her unquestionable support at all times, I would never have achieved the success that we both enjoyed. We shared good and bad times in equal measure, united in whatever life threw at us.

'Nothing gave her more pleasure than the visit to the Palace last year when I received our MBE, because without her understanding and tolerance, it would never have happened.

'We will all miss Sue very much, but at least she is now at rest and beyond further pain.'

CHAPTER 6

THE KINLOCH FAMILY

I was officially welcomed into the illustrious Kinloch family when I married Sue on 6 February 1971. I felt I was punching above my weight – her maternal grandfather was Sir Roger Backhouse, First Sea Lord and her father, David Kinloch, was a distinguished Commander in the Royal Navy, serving on the notoriously dangerous North Atlantic convoys during the Second World War, for which he was awarded both the DSO and an OBE. Before the war, he was an officer on *HMS Britannia* and tasked with keeping the Princesses Elizabeth and Margaret amused during their various trips.

Sue had three brothers, Michael, Charles and Colin, whose births at eighteen months apart happily coincided with their father's shore leave. She also had two half-sisters, Charlotte and Adria, and twin half-brothers, David and James.

Sue's parents divorced in the late 1950s, something which was almost unheard of in those days, so much so that her father had to resign as a magistrate and her mother, despite being the innocent party, was refused communion. As a devout believer and regular church attender, the hurt that sanction caused was deeply felt.

All four children were shipped off to boarding school between the ages of six and eight, as was the practice for many service children at the time. For Sue, this led to problems with feelings of insecurity, especially as at around the ages of eleven to fourteen she was sent to various relatives around the country during school holidays.

Sue's mother, Barbara, died in 1968 before I was able to meet her and I only saw her father once before he died a year later in 1969. It was a memorable meeting. I was introduced as Sue's current boyfriend and must have looked very awkward as I walked across the sitting room leaving dog excrement from my shoe on the beige carpet.

An upright and truly imposing character, the more he tried to put me at my ease the more nervous I became. He supplied me with a couple of stiff whiskies as we made polite conversation and on leaving, I was so confused I turned the wrong way up the dual carriageway. The only other person who has had that effect on me was HRH Prince Philip – perhaps it's a Navy thing?

Sometime after the separation, her father married his secretary, Judy, the mother of Sue's two half brothers and sisters. I have always admired Judy. Widowed at a young age with four children under five years old, she studied to obtain A-levels then took a teaching degree so that her holidays coincided with the children's. By the time she retired, she was head of English at the local secondary school.

Our wedding was held from Judy's house, which has been the family home for more than sixty years. There is always a warm and friendly welcome there and when we were younger, there was nothing Sue and I liked more than visiting Judy and her four young children whom, to this day, I can still make laugh with my stock phrases such as 'life was never meant to be fair.'

Sue was on holiday with Judy in France while I was with my mates in the South of France when I think we both realised that we wanted to be together. I am still convinced to this day that Judy had a hand in counselling Sue who, like me at the time, had no intention or desire to get married to anyone yet.

Of her three brothers, I knew Charles best, having worked with him for three years. During my courting days I often borrowed either his car or, more often than not, his wife Jill's car for weekend jaunts when one of mine was being repaired or replaced following yet another accident. Charles and Jill had two children, Alice and Tom.

In 1984 Charles married his second wife, Gilly, a bright, fun-loving art restorer who is brilliant at her job and has the most amazing memory for names and the people she meets. Always enthusiastic about life, she has been very successful in her profession and a great ally as a 'bolt-on.'

Charles was the one I went to for advice when setting up my first business in 1973 and Colin was a founder shareholder and investor when we formed the auction company in 1989.

When I first met Michael, he lived in a spacious flat in South Kensington with his wife, Rebecca before moving to Sellindge, less than a mile from our house. It's fair to say that Michael was not overly ambitious, but he was one of the nicest men I've ever met. He drove to London every day with Rebecca after dropping off his Labrador, Saffron, in the early hours to be looked after by Sue until their evening return, so we saw quite a lot of them.

After Michael and Rebecca split up, he moved to Bexhill where he met his second wife, Jill. They had three children, Tovah, Sam and George. Sadly, that relationship did not survive either and Michael got together with Chantelle and had two more children, Martha and Emily. He died in 2012.

Colin was very successful in the financial sector in London and lived with his first wife, Claire, and their three young children Harriet, Rachel and Alastair in Tunbridge Wells. Not long before he retired at the age of forty-five, he married Mary, a lovely, gentle person, with whom he enjoyed thirty-two very happy years until his death in 2020. They lived in Tenterden, just forty minutes from Bitford, so we saw quite a bit of each other over the years.

Colin was an astute businessman and really made his mark in Tenterden, where he became just one of twenty-five people to be made a Freeman of the town in the past 150 years. He was Chairman of the Day Centre, the local branch of the Conservative Party, the Parish Council and the Stop Tesco moving to Tenterden group, which delayed the branch opening for five years. When the shop eventually arrived, I wanted to send a Tesco home delivery van to his house with a bottle of champagne, but Sue managed to persuade me that such a prank would not be appreciated.

Always protective of her siblings' feelings, it was probably very wise advice.

I often joked with my six sisters-in-law how lucky we were to join the Kinloch clan, albeit as mere 'bolt-ons.' Over the years I have been asked to be best man, trustee and executor to one or other of Sue's brothers. Being the longest-serving bolt-on, I have adopted the fat old uncle role, speaking at many of the weddings, family parties and, more recently, at Colin's funeral.

Sue was never happier than when she was with her family. Her brothers were very precious to her and she saw them as substitute parents who were always there for her, as she was for them.

I have found that one of the benefits of adopting a new family is that there are no expectations of each other, few criticisms and no desire to give or receive uncalled-for advice. Or perhaps I was just extremely lucky marrying into the Kinloch clan.

CHAPTER 7

OUR HOMES

Sue and I were fortunate to be married before the rampant property price inflation during the mid-1970s, but buying our first house was still a struggle.

Our first home was a three-bedroom, detached house called The Grove, which we bought from the adjoining Sellindge garden centre in 1970, the year before our wedding. The house was of traditional brick and tile construction and needed total refurbishment. The location wasn't ideal as it fronted the A20 and was close to the railway track to the north, but it had the accommodation we wanted, a large garden with a small orchard to the rear and, most importantly, was just within our price bracket.

We paid £3,750 for the house, plus £1,250 for refurbishment, which was the first large contract for Barry, who has been a close friend ever since. Although now it seems cheap, the house alone was more than three times my salary and getting the necessary mortgage was far from straightforward.

Most of the furniture, some of which we still have, came from two of my parents' friends who were downsizing and the rest from auction rooms in Hythe and Folkestone.

We moved in immediately after our return from honeymoon and enjoyed three wonderful years there. However, by 1973 we had three reasons for moving. Becky was beginning to walk and we were frightened she might wander onto the busy road, which was the main artery from London to Folkestone; Sue, having moved into the area, wanted to live in a village where she might meet more people; and I was planning on setting up my own business, which would prevent me getting another mortgage until we had built up a track record to show we could afford the repayments.

A buyer was quickly found for The Grove at £14,000 and for just another £3,000 extra, we were able to move into Springville in the centre of Saltwood, a lovely village just two miles from Hythe. The house was stucco rendered and until we bought it, had been arranged as two flats occupied by twin sisters. The alterations were quite straightforward.

The downside to the house was that there was no off-street parking, although the long back garden adjoined a farm track to the rear. Had I been able to negotiate access tor a garage the price would have shot up, but to this day the garden is still landlocked.

Springville suited us well for four years, but on one side was a family with five teenage sons and on the other a couple who held a noisy, alcohol-fuelled party in their garden after the pub every Sunday afternoon. There was little peace and we felt it was time to move on to somewhere with no neighbours.

I noticed Smeeth Cottage was on the market through an Ashford agent. It seemed amazingly cheap at just £20,000 for a seven-bedroom, three-reception house in three acres and with a two-bedroom staff cottage in the grounds. When being shown round, the agent said we wouldn't be able to sell the cottage as it shared the rear drive of the main house. How wrong he was – we had a buyer at £13,500 within weeks of moving in. There were in fact a number of interested buyers and we chose Margot as our new neighbour, a delightful widow looking for somewhere safe and secure. She remained a close friend until she passed away some twenty-five years later.

The main house, which boasted a mahogany feature staircase in the entrance hall leading to a galleried landing, had a few structural problems and needed complete refurbishment. With the help of Mrs Fuller's son John, who was about sixteen at the time, I redecorated and painted the whole house from top to bottom and Barry installed a second bathroom between the two children's bedrooms.

Smeeth Cottage was a great family home but the upkeep was a challenge. We couldn't afford carpets throughout and Sue found the parquet and tiled floors a constant irritation with dogs and children going in and out all the time. The formal three-acre garden was almost a full-time job and the interior decoration occupied most of my spare evenings and weekends. When I was working on the house, I reckoned I should be relaxing and when I was relaxing, I had a conscience about not getting on with the work.

At a pub supper one evening Sue asked what I would feel about selling the house. I said that I'd be delighted as it was a millstone around our necks in respect of the upkeep inside and out, the business wasn't well established enough to employ anyone else to do the work, but I thought it was what she wanted. It turned out that Sue thought it was what I wanted – one of the rare occasions when lack of communication veiled our similar opinions.

The next day the house was on the market at £70,000 and it was with some trepidation that we told Margot we were on the move.

The idea was to move back into Saltwood, but with more space between the adjoining houses. Sue had said she would like to find our forever house rather than move every few years whenever I saw a deal in the course of my business. We found the perfect property at the same time as we accepted an offer of £68,000 from a London couple for Smeeth Cottage.

It came as a bombshell when we were told that the house we were buying in Saltwood was to be withdrawn from the market due to a domestic dispute. I didn't want to lose the London buyer, so we were faced with buying another house as soon as possible. However, there was nothing that appealed.

Coincidently, I had been asked to find a buyer for Bitford and a sale was proceeding to a Lady T from Aldington. The seller of Bitford, Mr Bonner, wasn't well and wanted to move before the winter. When Lady T made her offer for Bitford, I asked whether she had a house to sell and was told to mind my own business. When pushed, she stressed that she didn't need to sell her 'hise' to buy the new one. When I rang her to say that the contracts were ready for signing, I was told that she had not yet sold her own place. I reminded her that she'd said at the outset that she didn't need to, to be told 'only a fool would buy one "hise" without selling the existing "hise".'

I told Lady T that if she didn't buy Bitford, then I would do so at the same price of £48,000 but, obviously, not charge the seller commission. I was told to do as I pleased in the same indignant manner.

A week later she rang to complain that I had bought Bitford from under her and when I reminded her that I'd said I would buy it if she didn't, she admitted she'd thought it was a typical estate agent's lie, such is the reputation of my chosen profession. She was not amused when I replied that I did not lie because I was not titled.

Sue took some convincing that this would be the last deal before our forever family home. The plan was to move in and do a cheap refurb job while we looked for another house where we would hopefully move to within six months.

I didn't use Barry this time, but instead got in some real cowboy builders to do a quick makeover. We moved in on 1 January 1980 to find that the drainage didn't work and that the heating was broken. The dining room was stacked floor to ceiling with tea chests containing our belongings from Smeeth Cottage and much of the mahogany furniture had to be delivered straight to our saleroom as we were moving from a six-bedroom, three-reception house to one with three bedrooms, two reception rooms and a comparatively small kitchen.

All builder's merchants were closed over Christmas and the New Year so the builders couldn't arrange delivery of the materials until the second week in January. My parents popped down to see us and Mother declared it was no place for her grandchildren to live so took Becky and James back with her. Probably a good decision; if we wanted to go to the loo, we had to use the facilities in the pub next door. Little did we know when watching the builders do their lash-up that we would still be here forty years later.

We loved being in the country, and soon met farmer George and his son Stephen, who went to the same school as James, so we shared the school run. The house felt immediately like home with its 16th-century beams, two inglenook fireplaces and a stream running through the grounds. This time we didn't wait to agree that this was the place for us to stay for the foreseeable future and our first job was to redo all the shoddy work to our standard and set about making it into the family home that has served us so well. When my mother died in 1987, we added another bedroom and shower room over a larger hall so that my father could live with us.

Three years after we moved in, the farm next door was put up for sale. A local farmer wanted the land but couldn't afford the farmhouse that had been unloved for many years. We agreed that I would buy the farmhouse and the four-acre field between the two properties, which would enable him to buy the land. When he looked at the house, he saw only problems whereas I only saw opportunities, which is part of the DNA of an auctioneer. I subsequently sold the farmhouse for a small profit to my accountant and kept the field, which has proved a real blessing over the years.

Since moving in we have added a tennis court, seven garages for my car collection, a pool and converted the old annexe adjoining the main house into a snooker room. All the bedrooms are now also en suite.

I would add that I am not an advocate of an estate agent or auctioneer dealing and trading in properties, however above board and transparent. There will always be a public perception that something underhand is going on (and in many cases I've seen, they may well be right), which is why we have a strict rule that no directors or staff may trade or invest in any properties whatsoever apart, of course, from our own homes and the offices from which we work. It's often suggested to me that I must pick up some bargains in my travels, but with such an entrenched company ethos, there is no question of a conflict of interest either in respect of a buyer or seller.

In 1983, Barry bought a house on the Costa del Sol with a friend and invited us to use it at regular intervals. Despite being asked many times, Barry wouldn't accept any rent or even a contribution towards the expenses, which made Sue and I feel somewhat uncomfortable. I could understand Barry's point – the villa was vacant when we wanted it and he didn't wish to profit from friends. I feel the same when people come out in my boat; I find that most things are more enjoyable when shared.

After two years, the friend's circumstances changed and he wanted out. Understandably, Barry didn't want to sell so offered us, and two other frequent users, a share in the villa at no. 47 to replace his existing partner. We all jumped at the idea. It would give us an opportunity to use the villa while contributing towards the upkeep and reimburse the capital outlay of the original half-share owner.

The arrangement has lasted until this day with one or two shares changing hands over the past forty years. There are only two rules: that the house is professionally cleaned after each visit, whether for a day or a fortnight, and before offspring can use it, the week in question is offered to the other shareholders first.

When I decided to take life a bit easier, Sue and I spent more time at the villa. We offered to increase our contributions, but such an idea was unanimously refused by the others.

The villa is one of just ten on the front line and none of the others ever became available. Then, in 2007 no. 37, a three-bedroom villa just five doors down, was offered for sale by the executors of the original 1983 buyer.

The market in Spain was in the doldrums but Sue and I both thought it would be nice to have more space, especially as the children and grandchildren enjoyed the location so much. As the prices were falling, I was somewhat diffident, but Sue persuaded me to go ahead. The conversation went something like 'Sue, this is a crazy time to buy, prices are dropping like a stone,' to which she replied, 'Had we bought it last year, what would the situation be now?'

My response was 'Well, we would have paid too much but would now own it.'

How could you argue with the reply: 'Well, let's pretend we did that then.'

We have never regretted buying our own family holiday home while also retaining our share in the original villa. When the family are there, Sue and I often stayed at no. 47 so that we could all be together yet have much-needed space for the generations to do their own thing.

CHAPTER 8

FURNITURE AUCTION ROOMS

Auction rooms are fascinating places and were at one time surrounded by myths, which programmes such as *Homes Under the Hammer, Bargain Hunt* and *Dickenson's Deals* have succeeded in broadly dispelling since they first aired on TV in the mid-1990s.

When I left Heddle Butler, I rather thought that my furniture auction days were behind me. However, a former partner of the practice called one day to ask if I would sell a cottage and its contents that formed part of an estate of which he was an executor. This was something of a challenge, but he was insistent that now John was enjoying the heady role of MP, he wanted me to deal with the whole thing.

I duly rented the former sorting office at the old post office for a week and moved the furniture in for viewing and auction, having already catalogued it *in situ* at the cottage. I advertised the upcoming sale and was touched by the number of former clients at Heddle Butler who asked me to include some of their items as well. It all went well and after several requests about when the next one was taking place, a new addition to the business was created.

We held the auctions on Saturdays, thereby encouraging not only the trade but private buyers as well. They took place once a month in the former turkey sheds at Hayne Barn before I secured a longer lease on the old post office, just opposite my office in Hythe High Street.

The turkey shed was a redundant Atcost farm building – low ceilings, poor lighting and a long, narrow, cold room which leaked when it rained. Many an evening I went to place buckets in strategic places to catch the water; one of my buyers, an elegant, fun-loving lady, even wrapped her feet in plastic bags to keep out the cold when she visited.

An elderly couple from Tenterden, Mr and Mrs Watts, would buy all the china and glassware and sell it to the trade piecemeal. Seldom would they spend more than a pound or two per lot but boasted of doubling the price, showing a 100 per cent gross profit – more than the big buyers could hope for, apparently. How many times would I drop the hammer to 'Watts, a pound' to the retort from some wit in the room, '20 shillings, Mister!'

Before the internet, the ring was prevalent. This is the term given to a number of dealers who agree not to bid against each other in order to buy an item in the auction as cheaply as possible then have a 'knock out' later, when they share the profits based on when each withdrew from the clandestine bidding. Highly illegal, of course, but understandable when one thinks of them meeting on a daily basis at rooms around the county and reluctant to outbid one another.

It is the auctioneer's job to break the ring – either by protecting the lot with a realistic reserve, widening the audience so that the power of the ring is diminished, or outwitting the person nominated to bid on behalf of the consortium.

As long as there is a private buyer or one or two dealers who don't want to join in, the ring is ineffective. The downside is that with some specialist items, the ring will be guided by an expert in the field; if the expert shows interest it must be right, so they keep on bidding.

This can backfire. One of my regular buyers, Ron Godfrey of Sandgate, had no wish to be part of the ring – if he wanted something, he was prepared to pay the right price and if he missed it, so be it. On one occasion there was a good longcase clock (sometimes known as a Grandfather clock) in the sale. Ron bid up to £1,500 at which point he said 'no more' and left the room. As I was about to drop the gavel an old boy from the front row said, 'Excuse me – can I bid £1,700?' to which the answer was, of course, yes. He carried on in this diffident, time-consuming style until £2,500, when the ring said, 'He's a nutter – let him have it,' to which the old boy, again hesitantly, responded 'Mr Godfrey said can you put it on his account please?' Not a happy ring!

On another occasion we had a distinctly ordinary cat ornament and I opened the bidding at just £2. From the back Ron said, 'Mr Auctioneer, I have a lunch appointment – can we start at £25 or I'll be here all day?'

The ring was on to it immediately and the bidding stopped at £95 when it was sold to them, after Ron dropped out with a sigh. At the end of the auction they came running up to find that it was stamped 'Woolco' on the base and was indeed worth no more than the opening bid of £2.

I asked Ron what all that had been about when he came to collect his bits.

'Oh,' said he, 'they just wind me up sometimes and need teaching a lesson.'

'A dangerous game,' I ventured. 'What if you had been left with it?'

To which he simply replied, 'I like cats.'

With the advent of *Antiques Roadshow* everyone became an 'expert' overnight. If it was 100 years old it must be worth money. Into that category went treadle sewing machines, family bibles, standard lamps and the like. We didn't make much profit from the auction rooms, but solicitors and executors would give us the house to sell if we also cleared the contents.

We therefore quickly built up a pile of junk that needed taking in order to get the better pieces and, more importantly, the house sale. To store such items, we used outside sheds or, for the client's benefit, the 'external sales area.'

One day a flatbed truck came into the yard with a tatty chair on the back covered in a 1970s nylon burnt-orange cover.

'Oh God,' said Tommy the porter, 'shove it in the shed.'

The lorry driver was very grateful as he'd just been turned away from Butlers because they were trying to upgrade the lots in their room.

No more was thought about the chair. However, by this time I had been elevated to the ivory tower by Ward & Partners and a rather snooty ex-graduate with a degree in fine art was employed to manage the saleroom and catalogue the items for sale. The auctions were still held on Saturday and I continued to take the rostrum, having popped in to view on the previous Friday evening to acquaint myself with some of the more important pieces.

From the quality of dealers in the room there had to be something really special; qualifications in fine art are one thing, but experience is equally valuable.

'No,' I was told, 'it's just a normal household sale – nothing of importance at all.'

I looked high and low and, in the end, had to agree; perhaps a shortage of stock had brought out the big boys, however unlikely that seemed.

The way I got rid of those painful 'antiques' of little or no value stashed in the sheds was to hand over to a novice auctioneer. This would give the newcomer experience and if a bid was missed, the most at stake was 50p or a £1. The old ladies in the front row would feel sorry for him and buy all the tat as their good deed for the day and I would get a coffee break and get rid of the crap, ready for the next assignment. At the time we were selling 600 to 800 lots at 130 an hour (i.e., more than two a minute).

Keith Rogans, who joined me from school at sixteen and now runs the most successful estate agency in Hythe, was the rookie who drew the short straw that day and after his first ten lots I heard the familiar cry: '50p, Keith – be reasonable – I'll give you £50.' The bidding finally ended at £13,500 for the Queen Anne wingback chair, identified by just the ball and claw foot showing below its burnt-orange nylon cover. When put into context, the whole sale usually made between £3,500 and £5,000. So much for a fine art degree. That night the chair was swiftly moved to the main saleroom, where it was protected by the intruder alarm.

In those days, burglar alarms were somewhat temperamental and the police had a policy of three false alarms and you were on your own. To combat this, I had left a broken high-level window unrepaired so if we were called out, I would point to the window and suggest that some kids had thrown a stone through it.

All went well until I received a call at home late one Saturday evening that the alarm was ringing and would I attend. A friend having dinner with us thought this mundane routine was very exciting and asked if he could come along. When we got there, he was surprised to find that the key holder was the first to enter the premises, followed by a police officer some distance behind.

It was established that nobody was in the room so I accepted it was a false alarm, until I spotted the broken window – some kids must have thrown a stone through it, I protested. 'Hang on,' said my dear friend, 'if that is the case, where's the stone – and there's no glass on the floor?'

This was an observation that had eluded the bobbies on the beat on so many previous episodes and it was duly put down as a false alarm.

Whatever their role, each member of a team is as important as the next – something that I had to remind our fine art expert on more than one occasion. In the saleroom the porter is vital to the smooth running of the operation. He is the one who receives the goods and is responsible for checking them out. Theft seems like a game to some bidders, especially if they've missed an item and regretted it later. One ruse was to buy a wardrobe for a pound or two and then fill it with a few extra bits to sneak past the door.

Tommy, our highly experienced porter, was up to all the tricks and not much got past him. So, I was appalled to hear the auction room manager tearing him off a strip in front of customers over a silly matter, the importance of which she had clearly not learned at college. When we were alone, I told her that she was never to speak to a fellow member of staff in such a way again, to which the haughty reply came back: 'But he's only the porter!'

She didn't forget my response.

'I have a bad back – I can't do his job, but I can do yours better than you, so to me he is more important than you are.'

The message was received, loud and clear. However, Tommy asked me not to fight his battles for him again, adding, 'If she apologises to me just one more time, I'll punch the bitch in the face!'

Porters are an essential ingredient to a successful, efficient operation – literally the eyes and ears of the auctioneer. Get a good one such as Tommy and they are like gold dust; a bad one can be the rotten apple in the barrel which will reflect on the reputation and integrity of the whole business.

This distinction became evident when I was asked by a friend who owned a chain of offices in south London and Surrey to have a look at his auction room in south-east London and advise on the way forward. Apparently, it had been part of an acquisition he made many years before and run by a manager ever since, neither making a massive profit nor causing unnecessary demands on the management of the core business.

The manager had decided she wanted to retire and so I was asked whether the business was worth developing or maintaining. I duly visited one morning and in no time was concerned that there was definitely a fiddle going on – I just needed a little more time to establish just how big the problem was and who was involved.

I soon realised that the two self-employed porters were certainly part of the problem – it was just a matter of who else had their snout in the trough. Furniture auctions are made up of a number of items from several different sources; some are complete house clearances, others individual items and then there's everything in between. The method of knowing which lot came from where is to place an owner's coded identification sticker on each item to establish the provenance.

When I visited the saleroom I discovered a locked door to a store adjoining the auction room, but when I asked to see inside the store, I was told by one of the porters that the key had been lost. Alarm bells were now ringing loudly and there was no doubt that I was being lied to.

'I'm off to lunch,' I said, 'and when I get back I want the key found or I'll kick the door in – no excuses!'

When I did see inside the room it was like an Aladdin's cave of nice pieces, clocks, small furniture, Objets de Vertu, etc., none of which had an owner's label. What was evident was that during house clearances, especially in cases of probate, some of the better items were being put to one side and if a beneficiary asked where a certain piece was, they were either told that it was being reserved for a specialist sale or awaiting further investigation before cataloguing.

Once the bulk of the estate had been sold and no queries raised, the item was then free to be sold under a false name and the proceeds paid into the porters' nominated account. Theft and dishonesty at the highest level in my view – a disgraceful betrayal of trust.

I spoke to my friend that evening to advise of my suspicions but asked that he did nothing until I could establish who was involved. I did, however, mention as an aside that if he discovered the auctioneer was involved then he should be sacked and if he was not, he should have known what was going on. Whichever, he was not fit for the role. The conversation ended with my asking him to take no further action until I had revisited the premises to investigate further.

I could not believe it when he phoned me back the next morning to say that he'd called the auctioneer in and fired him on the spot.

'Well done,' said I, 'so who is going to conduct the 500-lot sale the next day?'

Silence.

'I didn't realise,' he said. 'Can you do it, Clive?'

'Sorry, no – I have a radio interview first thing.'

I then asked James to go to south-east London the next day, find the auction room, introduce himself and start the auction at 11am and I would be there as soon as I could. Something you could really only inflict on family.

James wasn't experienced in furniture auctions – he's dyslexic like his father and was entering a potentially hostile environment on his first auction at that venue. When I eventually arrived at 12pm I went up to the rostrum to take over. He turned off the mic and said, 'You can sod off – I've got this far so I'll finish it!'

The apple never falls far from the tree. I obediently sat outside in my car so as not to intimidate James by watching his every move. After all, if I thought he was good enough to start the sale I could hardly argue he was not capable of finishing it.

After a couple of months, the auction room was closed. The site was far more valuable than the business, which would have to restart from square one.

Back in the Hythe saleroom, the characters and their comments were legion and made auction days such fun. One of my buyers was a cockney who owned a house just outside Hythe, where he stayed with his wife and young daughter at weekends. He was, I later learned, an East End crook – hard to believe as he was such a laidback, easy person to deal with. If he wanted an item, and it didn't have to be particularly special, he would keep bidding until he outbid his opponents – whatever the price. Clearly, when you steal the money it doesn't have quite the same value as if you earn it.

Private buyers assumed he was a dealer and carried on bidding on the basis that if he was a dealer, they would save his 'profit.' The ring hated him, of course, as he outbid them on many occasions. Apparently, he ran a *Daily Mail* delivery service in the West End and had twelve vans running around London during the night delivering the papers for the next day – the thirteenthth van contained the acetylene equipment used for cracking open safes. If there was a road block the vans were waved past: result!

In those days my father, a brilliant mathematician and bridge player, did the clerking and accounts and he was also on the parole board at Maidstone prison. Imagine my dismay when he said he thought we could do without our cockney buyer as he was a big-time criminal and frequently mentioned by those seeking parole as the mastermind, the provider of shooters and the 'fence', the person who buys stolen goods at a discount and either sells them on or melts them down. Sadly, I didn't have to deal with the situation as I heard later that my lovely buyer had crossed another crook and was never seen again.

I am the first to admit that my knowledge of fine art, and paintings in particular, leaves a lot to be desired. To combat my ignorance, I drew on the goodwill of many local experts in their field to help me out. One such supporter was Harold Chapman, a man I liked and had enjoyed talking to ever since our first somewhat difficult meeting. His son Nigel dabbled in antique dealing in those days and tried to emulate his father, but seldom had sufficient funds to pay his bills. He once bounced a cheque on me for several hundred pounds during the same week that he'd also pulled the same trick on two other local auction rooms – a crime that was reportable.

I knew that his father was successful and indeed drove the only Rolls-Royce in town, a fact that was impressive to a young auctioneer making his way. I rang Harold and asked if I could pop in to see him and was welcomed by a firm handshake, a cup of tea and a piece of his wife Rita's cake. Having explained the problem of Nigel, he sat back, his hands crossed over his ample stomach and said, 'Let me tell you a story. Twenty-two years ago, I got pissed one night and gave Rita one – and for twenty-one years I have paid for that mistake, but no more. You see Clive, if he had a broken leg you would see the plaster and feel sorry for him – but when the problem is in his head you don't see it, do you?'

When he had finished, I said, 'Sounds like I'm on my own then.'

'Oh no,' came the reply, 'there are plenty more where you came from.'

Consequently, I phoned Nigel once again and asked him to return the furniture if he couldn't pay for it. I was told it was already sold and that he had spent the money – apparently, he had had a lot of calls on his finances – but he would 'bung me a tenner' and pay the rest one day.

I noticed, however, that the cheque was drawn on a joint account with his wife and that she worked and, presumably, got paid at the end of each month. I waited until the 28th and re-presented the cheque. Result – it was paid. Nigel was furious and came storming into the office shouting.

'You've banked my cheque!'

'That's what it is for,' I explained, 'it's how the banking system works.'

'But what about my tenner?' he protested.

'Money is a bit tight,' I ventured. 'How about if I bung you a fiver and the balance later?'

The look on his face was priceless, the tenner was repaid immediately and we agreed that our business relationship would end there and then.

We had a call one day to sell a house and its contents following the death of the owner. My first inspection revealed some oriental pieces and period furniture. Being totally out of my depth, I called Harold and said that I thought there were some quite nice bits and would he pop round with me to have a look. I collected him, still wearing his slippers – he was so large by then he couldn't see his feet let alone put on a pair of shoes – and we entered the house in Tower Gardens.

As we went into the sitting room, he turned his massive body around and around and exclaimed, 'There might be some nice bits?!' I was worried that I'd wasted his time. 'Far from it,' came the reply. 'These are some of the best pieces I have ever seen in this town.' The contents were the basis of my first evening fine art sale, to which others entered top-quality items and my brother persuaded Nick Bonham to come down to Hythe to see how the little provincial auctioneers operated. I am not sure that Nick was terribly impressed, but over dinner we found common ground and a friendship that has lasted to this day.

As my knowledge of paintings is zero, I used to load up my Volvo estate with all the pictures consigned to us and take them to Bonhams auction house in London's Montpelier Street. While Alex Meadows and his team looked through them to extract the ones that would sell better in London, Nick and I would go for lunch at the Montpeliano Italian restaurant next door. It worked well; in London, buyers tend to buy artists, but in the small auction rooms they buy paintings they actually like.

Sadly, the arrangement stopped when the Prudential heard about it and could not believe that we didn't have a legal agreement between us. I have to say that, over the years, not once did a client complain that their painting had been consigned to a London auction house to achieve a better price. Such an argument cut no mustard with the pen-pushers in Holborn, so my trips ceased.

Harold Chapman and his family remained good friends and we spent many happy hours together. In 1976, Sue and I were invited by Harold to join him and Rita at his livery dinner. It was one of the hottest days in the year and we cruised up to London in his air-conditioned Rolls-Royce. Rita had an array of rings on both hands, four of which she sold at the banquet – those two never missed a chance to do a deal.

On Christmas morning Harold would open the shop and offer his customers a glass of sherry and one last opportunity to buy a suitable present for their other half.

The prices were, of course, adjusted upwards for the occasion.

I understand that his son Nigel and youngest daughter Laura are both prospering, having moved north many years ago. Alison, the middle daughter, is highly successful, a true expert in her field of antique jewellery and has inherited her father's business acumen and kindness. When Jenny, the oldest daughter, died on the operating table in her twenties Alison adopted her two children without hesitation. She is also a regular contributor on *Dickinson's Deals* TV programme and runs a thriving shop in Hythe High Street.

My regular appearances on the chattels auctions rostrum ceased when the division was sold by Prudential in 1987.

CHAPTER 9

THE LORD'S TAVERNERS

The Lord's Taverners was founded in 1950 by a group of actors who drank in the Tavern during matches at Lord's Cricket Ground in West London. After a time, they formed their own cricket side and performed at charity matches around the country, raising money to give disadvantaged children a sporting chance.

In 1989, a few weeks after I had launched Clive Emson Auctioneers, I received a phone call from an estate agent in Tunbridge Wells asking if I would conduct the auction at The Lord's Taverners West Kent Regional Christmas Lunch at The Spa Hotel. I had already appeared a couple of times for the East Kent Region as guest auctioneer but had no idea that by accepting the invitation, it would be the beginning of an interesting and enjoyable association with the Taverners for the next thirty-two years.

As always, the lunch was well-attended with notable sporting and showbiz personalities, excellent speakers and a wealthy and philanthropic audience. The General Secretary, Anthony Swainson, was in attendance and he clearly liked my style that day and asked if I would consider becoming a member of the Taverners and possibly conduct more auctions in other regions.

I have no illusion that when the auction starts at such events, 80 per cent of the audience do not wish to participate, are scared of buying something by mistake and would rather pass the time chatting with their friends. The other 20 per cent are quite happy to spend their money to help fill the coffers. So, when taking charity auctions, I tend to get on with it and keep the audience amused with jokes and repartee, much of which is aimed at the donors of the prizes and the bidders.

Most amateur auctioneers, on the other hand, tend to bask in their moment of glory, persisting in trying to get a bit more from someone who has clearly reached their limit and consequently losing the audience, who then start chatting, preventing those who want to participate from hearing what is on offer. Result: disaster and loss of potential income.

I was duly elected as a member and became a favourite of Patrick Shervington, who took over as director on Anthony's retirement in 1991. It was a position he held for five years, during which time I was a frequent guest on the London circuit. My favourite was the City Branch held in the River Room at The Savoy. I did, however, feel a pang of conscience walking past the homeless people sheltering under the arches as I was entering a champagne reception followed by a fabulous dinner.

The renowned Taverners Christmas Lunch is held every year at the Grosvenor House Hotel in Park Lane. It must be one of the most difficult venues in which to sell. The room is massive and seats more than 1,000 on round tables of twelve on the ground floor, with more tables on the balconies above. Keeping that number of people quiet while trying to identify bidders so far away is a challenge for the most experienced of auctioneers. I took the auction a couple of times, but was always relieved when Patrick said he wanted to ring the changes and let someone else take the rostrum.

On a couple of occasions, I was asked to attend as reserve auctioneer, usually because when celebrities agree to attend a charity function it is on the understanding that if they are offered professional work then that should take precedence.

I shadowed Jeffrey Archer one evening at Grosvenor House and was impressed that he thought the auction prizes were a bit lightweight, so he phoned Ford and they donated a car. It is not what you know, but who you know it seems – or more probably, what you know about who you know. Jeffrey was on top form that evening and is probably one of the best charity auctioneers I have ever seen perform; quick, witty and excellent at dragging the last penny out of the audience, once he'd identified where the money was.

It was a memorable occasion for me as I took Becky, my daughter, and we were on a table with David Frost and his lovely wife, Lady Carina, together with Michel Parkinson and Ronnie Corbett. Not bad for a country boy. Becky and I later came down to earth with a bump when we spent forty minutes looking for the car parked in the bowels of the hotel.

On another occasion I was at the Christmas Lunch at Grosvenor House when Bunny Campione from *The Antiques Roadshow* was invited to do the auction. The audience was appallingly rowdy and Patrick had to leap onto the stage twice to ask for quiet and respect for a lady guest. So ungentlemanly in every respect and not a good afternoon for both Bunny or the Taverners. Selfishly, I'm so glad that he did not ask me to help on that day.

My son James kindly offered to collect me as we were both then going on to Birmingham for an auction the following day. He was held up in rush-hour traffic and when he finally arrived at 6.15pm, having had an altercation in the Mercedes with a London cab on the way, he was told that everyone had left apart from two blokes sitting in the Ladies downing a second bottle of champagne. Which is where he found Patrick and me, deep in unintelligible conversation. Luckily for James, I slept all the way to Birmingham.

At one of the lunches at the Hilton the auctioneer was to be Henry Kelly, who had a reputation for being difficult and they wanted me on standby to take over if he got out of hand. Why people doing a job they love for an unjustifiable fee get such a feeling of self-importance is beyond me. Everybody knows that at these large fundraising events the final toast is seldom, if ever, before 5pm.

I sat next to Henry and listened patiently to him telling me how popular and successful he was. Not once did he show any interest in me nor, indeed, why I was on the top table next to him. At 4pm he shouted abusively at one of the attractive female organisers that he was supposed to be on at 3.30pm, that the whole event was a shambles and that he had to be at rehearsal by 4.30pm.

'It's your lucky day,' I piped up. 'I'm a professional auctioneer here to take over if you kick off, so instead of being so objectionably rude to someone who can't answer back, why don't you just bugger off to your rehearsal and I'll conduct the auction?'

As always, when confronted, a bully will step back a bit. In this case he said that, on reflection, he might have been out of order and that he thought the rehearsal could wait a bit longer. Result!

Prince Philip was patron and 12th man in the Taverners, having been a keen cricketer in his younger days, often playing in small village grounds such as Mersham-Le-Hatch on the Brabourne Estate, a lovely, friendly village club of which I am one of the vice-presidents. HRH Prince Edward was President of the Taverners at a lunch held at The Dorchester, where I was conducting the auction. As one of the top table guests, I was presented to him in the green room. He struck me as being a lovely, kind gentle man and someone whom I have admired ever since he resigned his commission in the army. Telling his father of his decision must have been even more daunting than the inevitable speculation in the media. Bravery, not weakness, in my view.

As we were chatting, I asked him what the latest was on his newly launched film company, Ardent. He didn't quite understand the question so I asked him what his film company offered that the others didn't.

'Well, my Royal connections, I suppose,' came the answer. Note to self: avoid Ardent shares!

Having been introduced by the Master of Ceremonies, I started as usual with 'Your Royal Highness, my Lords, Ladies and Gentleman, could I ask for your attention for the next ten minutes when I will try to raise much-needed funds for our beloved charity?' As I looked down, Edward was still in deep conversation. 'Hey,' I called out to him, 'you're the only one I mentioned by name!' To my amazement, he blushed and apologised. Just imagine if I had said that to Andrew or Anne.

Through my involvement with the head office at Taverners I was asked to be Chairman of the East Kent Branch. In my view, it needed someone more high profile in the music and entertainment industry and I persuaded my friend and fellow Taverner Jo Rice that he was the man for the role. He did an amazing job and was a difficult act to follow when I took over from him as Chairman and eventually President.

It was an ideal set up – five members, each with their own skills. John Greenwall was a food connoisseur, Jo Rice was brilliant with music and bands, Phil Giles was treasurer and I have contacts for marquees, guest lists and organising large events. We were each allocated the roles at which we excelled and got on with it, no tedious meetings discussing the obvious as we all had complete confidence in each other. We held just three events a year – a Summer Ball, Christmas Lunch and a Golf Day, organised by Martin Hart.

John wanted to get the Taverners celebrity team to play cricket at Folkestone. In 2001 the deal was that to cover expenses, the region paid £7,000 to head office who then organised a crowd-pulling team. The £7,000 would be raised from a charity ball on the Saturday evening preceding the match and on the Sunday, where further funds would be generated by shaking buckets, holding raffles and selling autographs, etc.

John, having discussed the concept, reported that the Headmaster of the Harvey Grammar School was keen that the event should be held on the school's cricket square and left the bursar to liaise with us to organise everything. Three weeks before the event, we held a site meeting on the cricket ground to finalise the details. Only at that point did the Headmaster attend and wanted to know why we needed such a big tent for a cricket match. We told him that it was for the ball the night before.

We were spellbound when he stated quite categorically that under no circumstances would he allow a ball to be held on his grounds – it was surrounded by houses and would cause complaints. Surprising really, considering that the school often held such events. He wanted the cricket match but no fundraising ball and wouldn't accept that he had to have both, or neither. It took a little while for it to sink in that he could not have all his own way, Headmaster or not.

So, the committee was left with a dilemma; 250 tickets sold for a ball with no venue. The week before the match was to take place, my son James was to marry Kate and we had booked a marquee in our field at home. One quick phone call to James to establish that he would have no problem with us using their wedding tent ('I don't care what you do, we we'll be on honeymoon!'), followed by a second phone call to Jim confirmed that the marquee could remain for a further week at Bitford.

We cancelled the cricket match and saved £7,000. I was worried that people wouldn't want to venture seven miles into the countryside, but how wrong I was. It was a balmy summer night with the champagne reception in the grounds, stunning food and a great band that Jo had organised. This was the first of seven summer balls that we held at Bitford and we usually raised £20,000 to 30,000 every year from the ball, lunch and golf – enough to buy at least one Taverners bus for local charities.

It became a tradition that the day after, the committee would meet at Bitford for lunch to count the money and help clear up. This for me was the best part of the whole thing; relaxed, alcoholic and a laugh-a-minute.

Every year we were lucky with the weather, people swam in the pool towards the end of the evening in various forms of undress or in full ballgowns to cool down and the alcohol flowed. However, the various events were not without their problems. The band roadies were always demanding and on one occasion blamed a surge in the electricity supply for blowing a fuse and ruining their amplifier. They wanted £3,000 to mend it or they would go home. We established that they did, indeed, have another amplifier and that they should either use that or set off back to London immediately.

Paying £3,000 for an unprotected fuse seemed extortionate to me and when the roadie asked what we would do if they did indeed leave, my reply was not terribly clever: 'Not your problem. Either stay or sod off.' They stayed. Bravado at its best but I am still to this day not sure what Plan B was. It wasn't entirely reckless; the disco team was already there and could be persuaded to do the whole gig if it came to it. Not ideal, but far better than submitting to blackmail.

On another occasion, the caterer came over to me to say that John was having problems with one of the guests who wanted a vegetarian meal for his wife and if we did not provide it, he was demanding a full refund. Of the 250 tickets sold not one person had asked for a vegetarian option, but the caterers had set aside ten just in case.

The chap was getting quite agitated so I said to his wife, 'Come with me and I'll get you something from my fridge at home.' Of course, when I opened the door it was full of pies, sausages and burgers, but nothing vegetarian at all. The rather embarrassed lady apologised and said that her husband often did this to get a discount or refund. When we returned to the table, I asked him how much of the underprivileged children's money he thought we should give him. He blanched a bit before suggesting a total refund for both tickets. I pointed out that he had enjoyed the champagne reception, the food (apart from one portion of chicken for his wife), the band and the cabaret.

As he became more aggressive, I pointed out that it was not our fault that he hadn't ordered a vegetarian option, nor that his wife wasn't normal. When he asked what I meant by that I said, 'There are 250 people in here tonight and ten don't eat meat, so whichever way you look at it, it's not normal is it?' Fight fire with fire, I thought.

He was told that he could either have a free raffle ticket and take his chances or leave immediately with nothing. Sadly, when he applied for a ticket the following year, we were fully booked. I knew his Rotarian father really well, he's a reputable local businessman, and I couldn't help contemplating what difference a single generation and an over-indulged childhood can make.

The Summer Ball became so popular that on the penultimate year we sold 450 tickets. Sadly, however, the exclusive and intimate status was lost; we made more money but at the expense of some undesirables stealing bags and cameras from tables during the evening.

The following (and final) year we catered for 400, sold just 200 tickets and only 150 people came as five tables were cancelled at the last minute due to the England cup final that evening and one big and loyal party donor cancelled three tables due to a recent split with his wife.

We managed to reduce some of the catering costs, but of course the atmosphere was not the same in a marquee twice the size needed and we didn't benefit from the economies of scale in respect of cost per ticket to cover the band, kitchen equipment, provision of toilets, etc. The reduced attendance also had a dramatic effect on the bar profit, raffle and auction. To cap it all, when we sent in the return to head office which showed a small deficit, I got a call from a snooty schoolmistress-type asking if there had been a mistake and if not, what steps were we going to take prevent it happening again in the future?

I remarked that I couldn't remember a similar conversation the previous year.

'Did you make a loss then as well?' I was asked.

'No, we netted £32,000,' I said.

'Oh, we don't call if there is a profit,' I was told.

'Then don't bother me when there is a small loss,' I replied angrily. Did they not appreciate the sleepless nights and frantic phone calls over the previous weeks? And furthermore, we were not being paid like the central office staff – we were all volunteers!

That was not the only problem with head office. We got a call one year to say that we must obtain three quotes for the marquee in accordance with national protocol. This is where bureaucracy defies logic and local expertise. Having added £150,000 to their coffers over the previous five years, without any input from central – who couldn't even provide a high-profile speaker for the provinces – we were, effectively, being told that we couldn't be trusted to secure a good deal.

As with many other clubs and associations, substantial funds are raised from small voluntary regional committees. I explained that we only allowed one marquee company on our field, a company that we trusted implicitly, had worked with me for ten years and had three price lists: standard, discount and Clive's. No argument would suffice, so we got two further estimates from local companies, which confirmed that they couldn't get near our price.

Inevitably, Jim heard on the grapevine that I had obtained comparable quotes and that as the trust had gone and it was now a competitive tender, his price would revert to the standard discount, which was still below the competition, but some several hundred pounds more.

It took a lot of explaining and a few beers to convince him that I was just obeying orders and that our arrangement should stand. A quite unnecessary hiccup where so-called governance and best practice ignores personal contact, reason and local knowledge, but at least all the boxes are ticked even if it costs more. This was not my first encounter with charity governance, where those sitting up in the ivory tower lose sight of their obligations to the beneficiaries and the work in the regions.

As President and 12th man, HRH The Duke of Edinburgh hosted a most magnificent black-tie dinner in the Great Hall at Windsor Castle. I attended with three friends and as I drove up in the Bentley to the security gate, I realised that I had left all the passes and tickets in my coat back in the hall at Bitford. It took some talking to get us in, aided in no small way by the repartee from my passengers and the fact that our names and my car registration number were on the list. At £175 a ticket that could have been a costly mistake. Clare Teal was the cabaret act and the whole evening was very special and memorable. Without the Taverners it could not have happened.

I was involved with a local children's home and asked if I could help one of the youngsters acquire some cricket kit as he had been invited to play for a local team. Just the thing for the Taverners, I thought, whose motto is 'giving young people a sporting chance.' I rang one of my contacts at Buckingham Place and asked for help. I was told that the rules dictated that an application would need to be made by the cricket club.

I explained that my young man did not want everyone to know that he was in care and in need of charity; in every sense he wanted to start on a level playing field, so perhaps the rules should be changed. Oh dear, what a suggestion, just not possible. I did say that if this was not the ethos behind our beloved charity, I was not sure what else it was. I then rang Peter Ludgate, a good friend of mine and owner of Hubble & Freeman sports shop in Maidstone. 'I want to come and shoplift some gear from your shop,' I explained, 'but I need your help to choose what we need!'

As anticipated, Peter was more than helpful, kitting the young man out at well below cost. Three days later, I got a call from my contact at Buckingham Place to say she couldn't get what I said out of her mind. She had been in the cellar and found keeper's gloves, pads, even a cricket bat, all with Taverners logos, and that it was on the way. Naturally, I gave the young man the choice and he jumped at the Taverners kit – how cool and so much better than the other players would have.

Children in care seldom get such a feeling of being special. Peter had been so generous I didn't have the heart to tell him that his kit was usurped by a cooler set. At the next Taverners ball I offered in the auction a pair of unsigned wicket keeper's gloves. They went for £120 and when the buyer came to get them, he asked in a rather slurred voice, 'Who didn't sign them, then?' Alcohol does have its advantages.

For three consecutive years, Shepherd Neame, the oldest brewery in the country, offered the Taverners free use of their hospitality suite, preceded by a tour of the brewery. The dining room held eight tables of ten, one of which would be reserved for Jonathan Neame and his directors. The deal was that we kept all proceeds from ticket sales but would provide a celebrity speaker to entertain the guests. All the beer and three-course meals were gratis.

It shouldn't have been a problem for the Taverners, which is, after all, a club for showbiz and sporting glitterati. We had arranged for both President Bill Tidy and Chris Cowdrey to speak at the event, but Bill rang two weeks prior to say that he was really sorry but he was now unable to attend as he had to be in hospital that week. Three days before the night, Chris emailed to say that he had to go to a friend's 50th party that night – a diary confusion, perhaps.

So, once again, seventy tickets sold, an obligation to our incredibly generous hosts – and no speakers. I phoned a good friend of mine, John Shepherd, the former Kent and England cricketer and one of the nicest people I know. He told me that he had to be at a charity golf day but would get to us in Faversham as soon as he could. He was brilliant and made the evening a real success.

However, after three years we found it hard to sell the tickets as we were always fishing in the same pond and after a time guests are looking for a change. It was a real shame, but I have no doubt that another charity would benefit from our decision and appeal to a different audience.

In 1997 I felt that Patrick had been unfairly ousted over a dispute with the chairman; the director had become too popular and so had to go. Out of loyalty to Patrick, plus the fact that I had enjoyed five good years in the limelight and that the new regime now preferred high-profile celebrities as auctioneers for the London venues, I stepped back to concentrate on the regional auctions, of which there were many.

Make no mistake, the Taverners still does an amazing job in raising funds for disadvantaged children but I fear that the club atmosphere has been sacrificed for the corporate money-making machine and that the fun, at least at regional level, has been lost. It is now primarily a charity where the focus is on fundraising rather than a members' club where the fun and fellowship resulted in serious funds 'to give young people a sporting chance.'

Many of the stalwart members and I were extremely unhappy when the committee decided to sell the head office building at 12 Buckingham Place, London SW1 as the trustees had apparently been advised by the Charities Commission that it was inadvisable to have all your assets in one place. It was an unencumbered freehold bequeathed by a grateful member some twenty years earlier to secure the future of the charity.

Without consulting with the membership, the committee decided to sell the building for around £8.5million and rent offices deemed more suitable to administer a national charity at a reported £200,000 a year on a ten-year FRI lease. So that was £2 million gone in rent, while not only no capital appreciation but also a schedule of dilapidations at the end of the term made the whole deal senseless, apart from to a brainwashed committee, of course. And all done and dusted without reference to the members whose building it was in real terms. Baroness Rachael Heyhoe-Flint, Bob 'The Cat' Bevan and several other distinguished and ordinary members, of which I was one, tried all we could to get the deal overruled but were advised against a costly legal challenge.

I have to say that with the millions in the Taverners bank account, there are far more worthy charities desperate and appreciative of the comparatively small funds that we can raise where the donations go to the front line rather than line the pockets of a London landlord. Hence, the Golf Day which might have raised a paltry few thousand, also went by the board. It would be interesting to know if either the Lord's Cricket Ground or the Oval might have had spare office space that we could have used, but I wonder if they were even approached. The difference perhaps between entrepreneurs thinking out of the box and a committee listening to a quango.

It was the final straw that made me, and countless others, resign when it was clear that lessons had not been learned. Once again, without consultation, the Ladies Taverners were axed overnight, apparently to appease one of the woke sponsors. The Ladies Taverners were a vibrant organisation with their own logo and high-profile celebrities raising millions each year for the charity. Although transferred en masse to the Lord's Taverners, few, if any, of the former regional Chairmen and committee members were offered similar positions within the enlarged Lord's Taverners organisation.

So, the end of an era for me, but on the whole, a most enjoyable one – and all emanating from one charity auction in Tunbridge Wells.

CHAPTER 10

STARTING AGAIN

In 1989, I was forty-three years old, a regional director of a business losing £400 million, job opportunities were not in abundance and I'd also taken to heart the prediction of my geography master at King's that I was unemployable. I think I had proved that over the years.

The writing was on the wall at Prudential Property Services, so I decided to dictate my own timescale rather than wait for the business to fold.

The problem was, what next? I was not overenamoured with estate agency as a future career and besides, I couldn't see where I'd fit in to make a difference; the high streets were already overcrowded with estate agency offices, both large and small, corporate and independent.

My passion was auctioneering but, to date, every property auctioneer was part of an estate agency practice supported by a sales and management department feeding through instructions.

I tried to buy the surveying, management and auction division from Prudential Property Services as a package, but the message was loud and clear: we do not sell off parts of our business to existing employees.

So, the decision was to go it alone once again. I had talks with 3i venture capitalists and although interested, it was clear they wanted an early exit once the business was established. I would be back to losing control and seeing a business destroyed by the new owners.

Eventually, encouraged by Alan Milsted, I persuaded him and his son Geoffrey together with my brother-in-law Colin Kinloch, to invest in a speculative new business for which there was no precedent or track record. I had, of course, prepared cash flows and forecasts, but they did not take into account that one month after the launch we were to enter the deepest and longest recession in property since the war.

Peter Simmonds, a larger-than-life character with an enviable business acumen, was my manager at the Hythe branch of NatWest. When I spoke to him about the concept he was intrigued and liked the idea, despite there being no precedent of the business model to prove its viability.

Unfortunately, the whole project was nearly scuppered when a curve ball was thrown in by one of my friends. He was also an employee of NatWest and had moved from Folkestone to the commercial centre in Canterbury. He suggested I meet up with him as the commercial centre had more pull than a mere high street branch.

The next time I saw Peter he was holding a piece of paper and asked what on earth I had been doing. The report from the commercial branch was that they wouldn't touch it with a barge pole. It was with some diffidence that I asked Peter if this compromised the bank's backing.

'Certainly not, he replied.' 'I had some doubts about the venture, but as he hasn't made a good banking decision in his life, we will definitely go ahead.'

He also told me to choose my friends more carefully in the future. No love lost there then.

I did not mention the conversation to my 'friend' as there was nothing to be achieved and his wife and Sue spent a lot of time together. The potential damage had been done and disaster avoided.

However, when I was sitting next to him many years later at a dinner party, he said that he was so pleased the business was a success and had always known it would be. I quietly pointed out that disloyalty is one thing, but blatant hypocrisy is a step too far. He said that Peter should never have shown me the letter, to which I replied that he should never have written it. The subject was never mentioned again.

About three weeks after the launch of the new business in Folkestone, I received a call from John Stockey, with whom I had worked since taking over the auctions from Dennis Paulley at Ward & Partners in 1986. John was disillusioned with Prudential, as despite having worked my three months' notice, a new auctioneer had not been appointed. Indeed, the Monday after I officially left, I was offered a month's salary to attend for a single day to conduct the auction for which a replacement auctioneer had not been selected. John was understandably unsure of his future with the auction division so low on the management radar.

Hilary Harwin and the rest of the team also wanted to join me, which was a completely different plan to the one I had envisaged, but I was flattered by their confidence in the new venture.

After discussion with the founder shareholders, we decided to speed up the expansion, almost before we had started. We opened a branch in Strood so that we would be known as the Kent property auctioneers rather than the Folkestone auctioneer and it also suited most of the new team who lived in the Medway towns.

Naturally, the additional cost put pressure on cash flow and we decided to hold an auction in December rather than wait until February, which had been my initial plan.

Between the launch in October and the December auction the market had collapsed. It was the end of the double mortgage tax relief, interest rates had increased to 17 per cent, thousands of people could no longer afford their mortgage repayments and they couldn't sell because buyers were unable to raise mortgages at the new unprecedented levels of interest.

The prices dropped by 40 per cent – building societies and banks were repossessing at an unbelievable rate – and without the ability to borrow, negative equity was a serious issue for borrowers who, through no fault of their own, were holding unsustainable debts.

It took around a year for the repossessions to receive court approval and evictions took place around the country at which point the properties were placed on the market, hence the collapse. A classic case of supply exceeding demand.

Auctioneers were inundated with instructions from lenders who had no facilities to manage the houses and flats they had repossessed. Gardeners needed to be employed, the premises boarded up to deter squatters and with little or no demand, auctioneers were employed to establish the true market value. Borrowers were still responsible for the shortfall between the original loan, interest and costs and the eventual selling price.

Auctioneers around the country were blighted by a reputation for underselling properties. I cannot tell you how many conversations we had with people protesting that we were selling too cheaply, to which the response was 'Why don't you buy them then?' The reason was clear, they couldn't get the finance either. Banks and building societies had pulled down the shutters while trying to establish just how much exposure they had to the defunct market.

The first few years were a real strain. Costs were pared to the absolute minimum without compromising the business. We invested in advertising and promotion, second-hand cars were limited to £5,000 and bought from the local auctions, furniture, photocopiers and premises were all leased to conserve capital.

When I approached the printers, I said I wanted the same deal as Pru. I thought that with a specialist buying department, they must be getting the best price possible. How wrong I was. When the invoice came in for £20,000 for the first catalogue, I rang to say that we needed to get the price down quite substantially for future publications, otherwise the only people making money would be them. I was immediately told they could do it for £12,000 and when I asked why they had quoted £20,000, I couldn't argue with the reply: 'You said you wanted the same deal as Pru!'

I still had soft spot for the regional team at Pru; after all, it wasn't their fault that they were being thrown to the wolves. The finance director seemed unconcerned at my news of the price difference; apparently when the buying manager applied for their next job, a budget of £2 million would be more impressive than one of £1.5 million. So easy when it is other people's money and once again, I was reminded that I just did not understand how big business works.

I enjoyed the challenge of procuring goods and services at the keenest possible price – my mantra was 'every £1 saved is £2 we don't need to earn' and it has proved a valuable tool in the box during the various recessions that hit us from time to time.

I have forever been grateful for the support from Peter and my two founder shareholders. The original forecasts were soon history, more capital needed to be injected and patience in waiting for the business to take off was essential.

I am not sure that 3i would have been quite so understanding.

I think the support came from the fact that we could not have worked harder, no holidays were taken for three years and we were on duty most weekends when our competitors, mostly funded by large institutions, accepted the losses as a minor inconvenience. It was not their money and not, therefore, their problem.

The venue is very important and it took a lunch and much persuasion to convince the manager at The Great Danes Hotel that our auction would not have the same outcome as previously. In the early days of multi-lot auctions, the hotel was overrun with buyers and sellers, parking on the grass verges and causing inconvenience to the residents, hence a complete moratorium on auctions.

I explained that I was a small one-man band and that he would hardly notice we were there, and so our new home for Kent auctions was established. We agreed a daily charge of £750 against the list price of £1,500, which was the icing on the cake and achieved by my plea of poverty and an enormous amount of flattery about the qualities of the hotel and its staff.

In the early days we didn't have the luxury of boardmen and my son James, who was then sixteen, would help me load the horsebox early on a Sunday morning for us to travel from Thanet to Brighton to erect 'for sale' and 'sold' boards. We seldom returned before the late evening, tired and hungry.

The income was also bolstered by my working for other auctioneers. I was known as 'have gavel, will travel' and during the recession there were many companies able to collate a catalogue of repossessions, but no auctioneer to take the rostrum on the day. I sold for Stickley & Kent, Ashbury's, Christie & Co, Alliance and Leicester and many others.

The sales took place in London, Birmingham, Manchester, Leeds and Glasgow. I loved the opportunity – no involvement in the administration, marketing and accounts, just responsibility for the bit I enjoyed most, selling from the rostrum and being well rewarded financially. While I was gallivanting round the country, John, Hilary and the team were holding the fort in Kent.

As we were the only pure auctioneers not affiliated to or part of a chain of estate agents, the concept of offering a service to the 95 per cent of agents who did not have an auction facility was embraced from early on. There was no risk of the introduction leading to the agent losing other business conducted on behalf of the client and by becoming a joint auctioneer with us, they retained the client and received 50 per cent of our commission.

In 1989, everyone seemed to be vying for other companies' business; banks selling insurance, insurance companies selling holidays, estate agents selling mortgages, mortgage companies selling commercial loans, solicitors selling houses and so on. And banks, building societies and insurance companies had muscled in on estate agency, with varying degrees of success and failure.

We were crystal clear in our message – if it is for auction, it is for Emson – if not we will recommend a specialist in the chosen field. The concept was welcomed with open arms.

Many of the estate agency branches springing up were as a result of property professionals being disillusioned by the big corporations compromising service and quality in the name of profit. Many such agents were well known to me over the years and I was touched by the level of support I received from so many quarters. It was, if anything, a mini rebellion against the self-appointed establishment.

When we set up in 1989, we were in competition with six other land and property auctioneers in Kent, all of which had a separate auctioneering department. Today just one of those remains and their multi-lot auctions usually comprise no more than six to ten lots.

From early 2000 our biggest competitor was undoubtedly Ward & Partners, a new company bought from Prudential Property Services following their demise and rebranded to the well-known and respected name that was discontinued following their acquisition in 1986. The auctioneer was David Harvey, ably assisted by Kevin Gilbert. When David retired, Kevin took over.

They were formidable competitors and equally aggressive with their marketing – a real pain in the backside, in fact. On one occasion they sent round a circular stating that twenty-seven offices were better than one, which was actually quite a good strapline and clearly directed at us. We did a quick check and realised that we had several more than twenty-seven outlets throughout our joint agency network and that they were a part of it because they wanted to be, not because of a diktat from head office.

We contacted all our joint agents asking if they would like to become more involved by holding our catalogues, whether or not they had a property in the auction. Thus was born the unique relationship where now more than 850 agents are happy to host our catalogues and many have a Clive Emson poster in their window advising that catalogues are available and entries can be handled at the branch. So much for twenty-seven offices.

In 2004, I took Kevin to lunch and suggested that he join our company and work with dedicated auctioneers instead of a department in a large organisation where the focus was on the core business of estate agency. He declined, he was happy where he was, and left to get on with it and produce tidy profits.

Six months later he rang and invited me out to lunch. Was the offer still open? He had been refused a request for a three-week holiday to visit his relations in Australia, despite having sorted cover during his absence as it was against company policy. He managed to get close to the three weeks by including two bank holidays and some time off in lieu. On his return he found that the area manager had totally re-organised the department to be run on the same lines as the estate agency.

The timing worked well for me, as I wanted to stand back from day-to-day property inspections and appraisals and Kevin was familiar with my operational area. Their auction department staggered on for a few years, using the services of a consultant auctioneer who attended to take the rostrum but had little other involvement or interest. As with many large organisations, the commitment was just not there for non-core parts of the business, however profitable.

The beauty of being independent and working with auctioneers is that we are agile enough to make instant decisions. Too many times we've beaten other firms to the post while they are waiting for a decision from the main board, marketing department and forecasts calculated by the accounts director who is more interested in budgets than the business opportunities that have presented themselves. However, I am the first to admit that we have made some errors of judgement, which are recorded elsewhere in the book.

Although not having a diverse board of directors, we do constantly listen to successful business acquaintances on social occasions and act on suggestions on how to improve the performance of the company.

I was playing tennis with Anthony and Barry one Tuesday evening in 2002 after a busy auction. I mentioned that we had sold sixty properties that day, which meant 120 handwritten contracts. If there was a mistake whereby the memorandums differed in any way, the sale of that particular lot could be void and unenforceable. It was a serious risk, however many checks were made during the process. Anthony, who had developed the computer system for what became one of the largest holiday businesses in the country, couldn't understand why the task wasn't computerised. I looked round for a suitable package, but as there are so few dedicated property auctioneers there were none available.

We therefore employed a company to write our programme which not only dealt with the memorandums of sale, but also viewings, legal packages, standard letters to the lawyers, joint auctioneers and clients. A name and address had only to be typed in once and it would permeate throughout the whole system. An extremely expensive and time-consuming piece of software and after about six months and two-thirds of the way through the process, the firm we had employed went into liquidation. We negotiated to buy the source code from the receiver at a knock-down price as it was of little use to anyone but ourselves, despite having cost a small fortune.

At around the same time, my son-in-law Steve was made redundant when the shipping company for whom he was a computer programmer merged with a larger organisation. Steve decided to set up his own computer software and support company and accepted an invitation to complete the programme for us and manage our whole computer requirements. An excellent result for all concerned and Steve has, again, proved invaluable as we have adapted to online selling. Much of the equipment is bought from a local company where my daughter, Becky, has been employed since 1998. A truly family affair.

From the outset we prided ourselves at being ahead of the game and were able to introduce new methods with skill, speed and efficiency. The auctioneers are the owners and operators of the business. We were either the first, or one of the first, to introduce block viewings, publish guide prices, agree reserves at the outset rather than the day before the sale, book viewings and legal packs online, arrange buyer registration with pre-agreed deposits, have the full catalogue bound into the *Estate Gazette*, provide administration fees in respect of services purely for the benefit of the buyer, offer the services of an in-house publishing studio and in-house legal team to check the legal packs produced by the seller's lawyer, not to mention participation in *Homes under the Hammer*, corporate lunches and joint agent active participation, to name just a few benefits.

James joined the business in 1991, having left school to attend Harper Adams agricultural college. We were offering more and more lots in Sussex and decided to open a branch in Brighton in 2002 under James' direction. I deliberately held back my involvement in the new branch;

it was James' baby and his opportunity to establish his own branch under the Clive Emson banner.

Soon after opening Brighton, I received a call from one of my sisters-in-law asking whether I could have a word with my nephew, Sam, who was living in Brighton and apparently in some debt. I rang Sam and suggested a meeting. The debt was from his student days, it amounted to around £4,000 and was escalating as the bank was charging 27 per cent interest plus £20 a day for being over the limit, capped at £80 a week. At the time he was working for a pittance in a sports shop from 8am to 7pm. It was quite a problem for a young chap in his early twenties.

When I returned from the meeting, I rang my bank and asked for a new loan for Sam at the Emson interest rate and said that I would stand guarantor. I was told that that was not an option as they did not like family guarantors because of the embarrassment if the borrower defaulted. Maybe it's the cynic in me, but I reckon the real reason was that they preferred to extract extortionate interest rates from people who couldn't go elsewhere.

I told the manager that if that was the problem, then I would like to open a joint account with Sam with an agreed overdraft of £4,000, which would solve the dilemma. Same effect as a guarantor, but it ticked their boxes. When we got all the forms through asking for masses of information from both of us, I decided to send Sam a cheque to pay off his loan and let him know the affordable amount to pay me each month. He was told that if he defaulted or could not pay one month, I wanted to be the first to know and that I would break his legs. Same sort of terms as the bank, just different rates!

The point of this story is that some months later we suspected the manager at Brighton of defrauding us by diverting the commission on pre- and post-auction sales. I asked Sam to join the firm as an assistant at Brighton to hold the fort once we had caught the manager and sacked him. Sam was paid a higher salary than he was earning from the sports shop and provided with a car. He took to the job like a duck to water, possessing all the qualities: a nice smile, totally trustworthy, bright, committed and a hard worker. He is charming with the clients and is now a director and an invaluable team player, helping James, especially since the whole business went online due to the Covid epidemic. And all from one phone call by a worried mother.

From the time we opened the Sussex Office, I have taken the Brighton rostrum only twice, once at James' invitation as he needed to be on the floor for a particularly difficult client and the second time when he lost his voice.

Since then, James has been directly involved with the regional expansion, which now stretches from Essex to the West Country. In 2008 he was appointed managing director, since when the business has gone from strength to strength, ably assisted by a loyal team.

We have never really planned the expansion that has taken place, as for a new branch to be successful it needs a good, experienced local team to run it. Unlike retail, we cannot buy in the lots wholesale, each instruction is obtained by virtue of reputation and the seller having confidence in the representative we send to evaluate the property and establish if it is suitable for auction.

Rob Marchant was planning to set up a new auctioneering business in Lee-on-Solent in Hampshire and was advised to give us a call first. When we met it was clearly his ambition to go it alone, although together there would have been the advantage of an established name, inclusion in the *Estates Gazette* and the economies of scale. Had he joined us on day one I knew he would always wonder whether going it alone might have been a better option.

My advice to him was try it on his own and if it proved a success, we would have to fight him for the lots if we wanted to go westwards. On the other hand, we would be there if he wanted to join us at a later date. Two years later we got the call that he would like a chat. It was lonely on his own; he was, as I knew, undercapitalised and wanted to join forces.

We acquired his company in 2004, refurbished his offices, bought him an upgraded car and invested in professional signage. We eventually moved to more suitable premises in Fareham and Rob has run a profitable branch ever since, with his son Michael and a loyal team to help him.

The journey further west to Exeter was a similar story. I knew Graham Barton from *Homes under the Hammer* (he's the one with the stripy jacket) and he rang me to ask how much it cost to set up an auctioneering business. We decided to meet in Maidstone and he went through his figures with James and me. Apparently, he was fed up with Countrywide as he had just had one of his most successful sales, but was hauled over the coals by the area manager for not meeting the mortgage or solicitor referral targets.

It was apparent from his presentation that, although a good auctioneer with a respected local reputation, his business acumen left a lot to be desired. It was agreed that he would open a branch in the West Country under the Clive Emson banner in 2010 and he brought two of his team with him.

The Essex office was in a similar vein. Again, Countrywide had decided to close their Chelmsford office and relocate the team to either London or Birmingham. James knew the manager, Paul Bridgeman, from serving on the NAVA committee with him and expressed surprise at receiving a text to say that he was moving on and would furnish the new contact details in due course.

James was on the phone to him immediately to see what the problem was and asked why Paul had not contacted us before making other plans. Paul reminded him that we had always said we were not interested in going to Essex, but James mentioned that it was only because he was there and we might struggle against a proven auctioneer with local knowledge, contacts and a good reputation. As I learned from the Ward & Partners days, it's the team on the ground that makes or breaks a business.

Within three days, the decision was to open in Chelmsford in 2015 and take as many of the Countrywide team who did not wish to relocate as possible. We have never regretted that decision. Yet again, Countrywide's loss was our gain.

I have always valued our staff, as without them, we would not have a business. James and I meet each one of them on an annual three-day round trip starting in the West Country on a Monday morning, having travelled down the evening before, and ending up in Essex on the Wednesday evening. One of the most important questions we ask is, 'How can we improve our business and what do you like least about your job?' The suggestions from the team members on the coalface produce amazing results and are usually introduced within a week, on the basis that it's no good asking the question if you then ignore the answer!

In the summer, all members of staff are invited with their families to a barbecue at Bitford, where the directors do all the cooking and look after them. Nearby hotels are booked for anyone who wishes to stay locally overnight. It's an ideal opportunity to mingle together and for us to show our appreciation not only to the people who work for us, but also to their families who support them when staying late or covering extra viewings over the weekends.

So, from the embryo of an idea in 1989, we now have a business which is within the top five property auctioneers in the UK and ranks as the leading regional property auction company in the country.

The sad thing is that I am not sure it could be done these days. For a start, there are no longer bank managers like Peter, able to make a decision based on knowing a customer and furthermore, a new venture will be faced with a minefield of rules and regulations that need a whole department to find the way through, making the initial set-up costs prohibitive.

CHAPTER 11

HOMES UNDER THE HAMMER

At the turn of the century, daytime television seemed to be dominated by cooking, gardening and antiques programmes. Many companies approached us to find a formula for a property auction programme and I wasted hours with over-enthusiastic researchers who suggested formulas that were either completely unworkable or gave a totally wrong impression of how the auction process actually works.

These included: 'Let us know when the buyer first views and we'll send a camera crew to film their first impression' and: 'We'll plant a potential buyer in the room and then they have four weeks to decide whether to proceed.' The response was, of course, if we knew who the buyer was on the first viewing, we could just sell it to them and avoid the hassle and costs of holding an auction.

The most important issue was ensuring that national television didn't give the impression that the highest bidder could withdraw from the transaction, thus defeating the message that when the hammer falls, the deal is done – there is no going back either by the buyer or, indeed, the seller.

One of the main benefits of an auction is not only to establish the true market price but also the certainty that the deal will go ahead, unlike private treaty (the more traditional method) where two to three months after making an acceptable offer, either the buyer or seller can decide whether or not to proceed to exchange of contracts.

It was, therefore, a breath of fresh air when Mel Eriksen from Lion Television rang with her concept of how a programme could be made, one that would not only give a true reflection of how property auctions work, but would also be entertaining and have longevity. She had clearly been to a few auctions herself and understood the process, so together we discussed how to put the ideas into practice.

The main stumbling block was filming the initial viewing, when the eventual bidder could not be identified at that stage. With a 100-lot catalogue, there would be from 200 to 300 fixed viewings, plus extras to accommodate people unable to attend the block viewing. There was also the issue that many people would simply not want to be on film. Having a camera crew on view days was not, therefore, an option.

We came up with the idea that once the hammer fell, the buyer would be asked if they wished to take part in the programme and if so, we would revisit the property with them, remove the sold board, re-erect the for sale sign and watch them come down the road as if on their first viewing.

This had the advantage of filming only the properties that were actually going to be featured, thus avoiding the initial visit dilemma. In the early days the auctioneer would also be interviewed as if this was happening before the auction, but in reality after the sale, to explain the interest in the property, what type of buyer it might appeal to and the likely price. Of course, this made me sound unbelievably clever, but with the hindsight of who bought and at what price, the speculation was spot on. Nevertheless, I did get a few comments and jibes about how the published guide price was so wide of the mark when I could predict the outcome with such accuracy!

The interviews were quite fun and relaxed. The recording team would arrive from London to set up the equipment in our office. Some were real luvvies – I mean, who wears a straw hat in the middle of winter? I was reminded on many occasions that this was all costing money and to take it seriously and that when asked what kind of buyer would get the particular lot, the reply 'a blonde-haired lady in a green coat on the right-hand side of the room' was not particularly helpful.

In early June 2006, Elton John headlined a concert at the St Lawrence Cricket Ground in Canterbury, which I was lucky enough to attend. The next day the Lion team arrived to do the post-auction recording and while they were setting up, I asked if any of them had been at the event the night before. Of course not -–they were all from London!

I mentioned that I thought Elton was brilliant, especially bearing in mind he had just broken up with David Furnish.

'Really?' they cried in unison.

'I thought you would have known, coming from London,' I teased, then delivered my punchline: 'Elton didn't like him having sex behind his back.' Laughter all round, and the filming began. A joke of course, but one that made them laugh.

'Tell me about this flat in Sheerness,' I was asked, '£40,000 doesn't seem much.'

Explaining that it was in an area where the houses were on wheels and the cars weren't, that it was above a fish and chip shop and the front door was approached through the back passage, I suggested Elton could have bought it. Again, laughter all round – plus a reminder that this was costing money and a retake would be needed. I went through the same reply, absolutely straight-faced, but when I got to the bit about access, the camera man burst out laughing. The third take was interrupted when the sound recordist's laugh was caught on tape. At that point we decided to move on from Sheerness and the flat never did feature on the programme.

Mel came up with the inspirational idea of having two cameras in the auction room, one fixed on the rostrum and a second roving camera picking out the various bidders. There would be a 'dead' area on one side of the room for those who didn't want to be filmed either because of shyness, they didn't want people to know that they were in the market or, more likely, they were with someone they shouldn't have been with. The roving camera was usually manned by Max, who we got to know really well. He could read the room and attended most of the other auction sales as well.

Homes Under the Hammer is an hour-long programme and manages to hold the viewer's interest by featuring three different properties in different regions around the country, thereby appealing to the whole BBC audience. So many people tell me they watch either when they're ill in bed or doing the ironing.

Initially there were just three auctioneers involved, Graham Barton from the West Country who always wears a stripy jacket, Graham Penny from the East Midlands and Clive Emson from the South East. We were each the leading regional auctioneer in our operational area. As the programme became more established and the viewing statistics recorded it as the most popular daytime show, more auctioneers clambered to be involved. The recognition impressed me, until I spent a few days ill in bed myself and saw the competition.

Following the telephone competitions scandal, where people were charged but then not entered for a particular event/prize, the BBC decided to clean up its act. Post-auction viewings and interviews where buyers were interviewed about their intentions regarding the house they'd already bought were stopped.

The annual lunches in London to thank the auctioneers for their participation were also sadly brought to a halt. They were a good way to relate to the other auctioneers in the programme and because of the annual contact, eventually led to Graham Barton running the West Country operation under the Clive Emson brand.

At the autumn sale in 2019 I was handed a list of phrases that could not be used on television, including 'ladies and gentlemen' as apparently the reference might offend non-binary viewers or those in transition. The room was a bit quiet by Lot 10, which is not unusual as we usually offer about five lots of ground rents in a row which are only of interest to a limited number of specialist buyers, generally on the phones or bidding by proxy.

To liven the room up again, I asked the audience if they had noticed how politically correct I was being. Max turned to me and said, 'Don't do it, Clive' as James started sprinting from the clerk's desk. But I was on a roll – 'Have you noticed that I haven't called you ladies and gentlemen, as there may be some of you who are not sure which, if either, you are? Until I read the BBC list, I thought LGBT was a sandwich.'

The audience of well over 1,000 was laughing – no complaints from the room but yet another piece of film on the cutting room floor. As with so many things, the 'woke' pendulum has swung too far and will continue to do so if we are all scared to have a view on any aspect of life that might offend a tiny minority.

As a company we feature at least once a week, more if you count the repeats and broadcasts round the world. I often see people staring at me in restaurants, trying to place where they know me from – especially in Spain where the ex-pats watch TV wall to wall wondering how things are going in Blighty. If it's like that for me, with just a cameo part, can you imagine what it must be like for the presenters Lucy Alexander and Martin Roberts?

I was in a taxi going to the Dorchester one evening and clocked the driver looking at me in the mirror.

'Give us a clue,' he said.

'I'm an auctioneer, you may have seen me at a charity do or perhaps on *Homes Under the Hammer.*

'Good for you,' came the reply. 'Front door or back door of the hotel?'

I suppose I deserved the put-down.

Unless it involves cricket, rugby or tennis, the BBC are fanatical about product placement. The cameraman is instructed to take angles that exclude all or most of the participating company's logo to avoid free advertising. I think all auctioneers play the game of having big signs posted around the room and dwell on a bidder standing next to one of them as the camera pans round. The bidder's number is also on a card with our logo.

Sometimes they need to be reminded that we are not paid by them and that our priority is selling the lots on behalf of the clients who do pay our fees. On the other hand, I am conscious of the value of being on mainstream TV, especially if the viewers know who we are.

As with most things, the better known you become, especially on TV, the larger the chance of fame biting you. One such incident involved the Trading Standards Office. In 2007, three months after buying a block of five flats in Dover, the buyer complained to Trading Standards that the property had been mis-described as 'refurbished'. A preliminary interview was arranged with Kevin and me at our office, then we were summoned to attend an interview under caution at their office in West Malling, where we were asked if an average person would consider that the premises had been refurbished.

When asked what they meant by an 'average' person and 'refurbished,' the questions took a different tack. I did point out that in my view an 'average' person wouldn't buy a block of five flats in Dover without inspecting them first, nor wait three months before actually visiting. Much can go wrong with a multi-occupation building during the eighteen weeks between our inspection and the complaint. We subsequently received a letter saying that no further action would be taken against us, but there was also a list of recommendations, which I circulated to all our negotiators.

I thought the matter was closed until I received a call from the BBC saying that the complainant had received a letter from Trading Standards saying that we had been cautioned and he thought we should not be featured on the programme. We were taken off the air with immediate effect. I rang the officer, explaining the serious consequences of his ill-judged letter, and although he agreed that we had not in fact been cautioned 'it is what it is and that was that' --his letter, although wrong, would not be corrected.

With such intransigence, I had no option but to leave a message with the head of Trading Standards asking him to call me. On the second call I was informed by the receptionist that he was too busy to speak to me. I asked her to tell him that if this was not addressed as matter of urgency, we would be suing his department for half a million in damages. On the third day I left a verbatim message to the effect that her boss was not fit for purpose and clearly promoted above his abilities. It took less than five minutes for this extremely busy man to ring back to object to my message. I told him that if I received a call saying that we were to be sued for half a million pounds I would regard it as a priority, if only to establish that the caller was a nutter. The difference was that it was not his money.

When I explained the value of twenty minutes on prime daytime television two or three times a week, he took me seriously. At the next meeting with him and the officer from West Malling, the boot was firmly on the other foot. Trading Standards are there to monitor wording and accuracy in advertising, yet failed miserably with their own correspondence. An apology was accepted in good grace and a letter was pre-agreed before being sent to the BBC stating that there was no case to answer, that we had done nothing wrong at all and that the matter was now closed. It was a stressful week with so much at stake, and all because of sloppy wording by someone who should know better and a less-than-clever buyer with a grudge.

How could anyone guess that from that early conversation with Mel how the public perception of auctions would change so dramatically? Until *Homes Under the Hammer*, the general view was that only distressed properties with problems were put to auction and only dealers bought and sold through this method. There was also a myth of secrecy, which is exactly the opposite to the reality of total transparency.

Since the first broadcast in May 2003, there have been more than 1,000 episodes of an hour long every weekday on primetime BBC television. The public not only feels involved, but now appreciates that the auction room is for everyone, whether dealer, private buyer and seller or trustees and statutory authorities, all wanting to ensure that the best price on the day has been achieved and for everyone to see that.

CHAPTER 12

PROPERTY AUCTION ROOM MEMORIES

My introduction to property auctions began in 1965 at Geering and Colyer, when I was involved as a very junior assistant in the sale of Rumwood Court in Langley, a magnificent Elizabethan mansion set in twelve acres and once owned by Lord Rootes.

It was a single-lot sale held at The Royal Star Hotel in the centre of Maidstone. I found the entire process stimulating and a good introduction to the whole theatre of property auctions.

In those days multi-lot sales were unheard of. It was a much more intimate affair, with the client, auctioneer and solicitor enjoying a lunch together before the auction to discuss the reserve and marketing response. Back then there was more trust between the client and their advisors; sadly, this has eroded over time as more dubious characters on both sides have entered the arena.

We sold a few lots at Heddle Butler in Hythe, again just one or two entries per auction, which were usually held mid-afternoon at the town hall. The auctioneer would read out the whole catalogue and conditions of sale and then invite questions from the floor before asking for the first bid. Having hired the hall it was understandable that they wanted to make good use of it, rather than find it was all over like a damp squib within five minutes.

Asking for questions was something I never really understood as I have yet to hear a question that enhanced the value of a property. It was instead an opportunity for the potential buyer to ask a last-minute question designed to put other buyers off, as they couldn't check the validity of the answer.

It also challenged the auctioneer and his knowledge of the property. Questions such as 'Is the right of way across the garden often used?' or 'Does the gate in the fence mean that the neighbour has a right of access?' are just a few of the red herrings I have heard posed.

The experienced auctioneer has a way of dealing with such questions, as well as hecklers from the floor. On one occasion, as the auctioneer was about to offer a cottage for £80,000, a voice from the back of the room called out: 'Moy father sold that coddage eighteen months ago for forty thowsand poand.'

Without hesitation, the auctioneer retaliated, 'I would imagine that was the second major mistake of his life.' What a put-down.

The same auctioneer, when confronted with a heckler from the audience butting in to say just before he sold a property in Headcorn that 'planes are flying over that house all day long' replied, 'At least they are ours.'

With multi-lot auctions, questions from the floor are not invited for three main reasons: the time it would take to address the potential hundreds of questions, the fact that the auctioneer may well not have handled the marketing of that particular lot and, most importantly, that no question is likely to benefit the seller's position.

It does take some of the drama away from the auction, but as any answer or statement from the rostrum forms part of the contract, it also reduces the liability of the auctioneer.

Just after I set up in Hythe in 1974, I was asked to sell a cottage (and its contents) by auction for the executors and at the same time a shop in the high street and five former airforce houses in Hawkinge. Together with three parcels of land it made a ten-lot auction, which was almost unheard of in those early days. We sold all but two of the houses and reported an immediate success.

I did not, however, get into the really large multi-lot auctions until I took over the reins from Dennis Paully in 1986. The Ward & Partners and Prudential auctions grew to eighty lots or more in no time at all and were held quarterly, raising well over a million pounds per auction. The sales these days are nearer £20 million.

When I started again in 1989, we increased the number of auctions from four to seven a year, the extra three promoted as interim sales. They now all have a similar number of lots and equivalent realisations.

At first I conducted the whole of the auction from the rostrum but after a time when the market eased a bit, John Stocky shared the podium with me, thus removing the danger of a potential catastrophe if I was taken ill or lost my voice on auction day.

To train a new auctioneer – and we now have seven in the company – I always took them to see Graham at a GA auction to demonstrate how not to do it. He never let me down. He would start off by saying that while on the rostrum he was more powerful than God and what he said was final – all of a sudden, he had 500 people testing this new deity. It would not be long before he would offer lot 35 – sorry, lot 49. He had two numbers on his page, the lot number and the reserve and I could always guarantee he would pick the wrong one at least once per auction.

It was Graham who rang me to say that the Great Danes Hotel wanted to increase their daily hire charge of £2,000 by £500 and that we should insist on paying the £2,000 and no more. At the time I had agreed £750 for the day. I told him I thought his company should pay the extra; it was good value as a venue and if I'd wanted to join a union, I would have gone into industry. He accepted that with good grace and when I phoned the manager to try to get a further discount, having enticed Graham to pay the extra, I reluctantly agreed to continue at the £750. All to do with communication, tempered with a bit of cheek.

Managing an auction room with up to 1,500 attendees can be a challenge. Most consider themselves to be knowledgeable about the process; in fact, when it comes to property everybody is an expert apart, of course, from those who practise it on a daily basis!

One of the issues is identifying the bidder in a crowded room, especially if they are standing in a direct line. In such circumstances, it is the auctioneer's duty to ensure that the bidder has been identified before dropping the hammer to avoid a later dispute. Once, I announced I was selling to the man in the green tie and after the hammer had fallen the under-bidder, wearing a red tie, came up insisting that he was the buyer. I mentioned that I had specified the buyer by the colour of his tie, to which he said he was colour-blind and what colour tie had his wife given him that morning? My reply was, 'Sadly, the wrong one!'

It is a bit of a game with some buyers to hold back until the last minute, raising their hand as the hammer is coming down. I do explain at the outset that the fall of the hammer is the exchange of contracts and that if they miss it, they miss it. If the auctioneer reoffered the lot because of a 'dispute,' we could be there all day with people who had just missed a lot having second thoughts after the hammer had dropped.

I was selling a ground rent for a local authority based on the Kent coast. The commercial building had been erected at his own expense by the tenant, who had been offered the freehold but thought that the £10,000 price tag was too high. After six months of failed negotiations, the lot was put to auction to establish its true market value. Amid the fervour of the room, bidding flew up to £95,000 until just two people were left, an investor from London and the tenant.

The tenant was being advised by a car dealer who said he knew all about auctions and convinced the tenant that I was 'running him' and to stop bidding. The London buyer bought it and the tenant claimed I had missed his bid. The solicitor for the local authority came to the clerk's desk to instruct that the lot was to be reoffered, as there was a dispute.

James told him that there was neither any dispute nor misunderstanding and that it would not be reoffered, at which point he reminded James that 'he was the solicitor,' to which the reply came 'and Clive is the auctioneer, which takes precedent in this environment.' The problem is that local authorities, and indeed nearly all statutory bodies, are scared stiff of a complaint from the public.

Shortly after this I introduced bidder registration, something that the London auctioneers didn't take up for many years. Registration took time and at first was resisted by some of the buyers, but it was so much better in all respects. Firstly, I would read out the paddle number before the fall of the hammer – no confusion there; secondly, we knew who the underbidder was in case of a problem; thirdly, the buyer could not 'do a runner' as we knew who they were. It also speeded up the paperwork as immediately on the fall of the hammer, the team could begin preparing the memorandum of sale.

All salerooms now register the bidders as it is a requirement of the Money Laundering Act. As usual, we were there first.

As soon as a new catalogue is launched, the two questions we get asked most frequently are: 'Will the owner sell it prior?' and 'What is the reserve?' The main reason an owner will sell prior is because he feels that the bid is greater than he might receive in the room, whereas the buyer wants it prior to the sale to knock out the competition and get it cheaper. As auctioneers we can gauge the interest from the number of enquiries, viewings and legal packs. Despite advising against it, clients will sometimes rely on their solicitor to make the decision and we are told that they have now sold it. We still get paid, but nonetheless, it is sad to see a client lose out due to poor advice given without knowledge of the full facts.

The answer to 'What is the reserve?' is: 'Tell me your maximum bid and I will tell you if you have a chance.' It becomes clear that the owner's minimum expectation and the buyer's top bid should remain confidential.

One of the games buyers play is to not bid when the lot is offered in the hope of buying it afterwards at a lower price post-auction. Seldom does such a ruse work, firstly because the seller has set his lowest price to attract buyers and secondly, you only need two or three buyers with the same idea coming up afterwards and then a second mini auction starts where, more often than not, they will pay more than they might have got it for in the room.

The magic of the saleroom is the prices that are often achieved and which exceed all expectations. A solicitor rang me to say he was winding up an estate and that it included a one-acre plot of shingle in the middle of the beach at Dymchurch. The probate valuation was £500 and he realised that the costs would exceed the sale price. As it was one of his established clients, he asked if we could do a deal on the expenses and commission. As a gesture of goodwill, I agreed to split the sale price 50/50 and take a chance that it might make £1,000.

The night before the sale the lot was featured on the *South East Today* television programme and a lady from Ashford thought it would make a nice present for her grandchildren. Also in the room was the land agent from the Ministry of Defence with orders to buy it as it was within the path of their firing range. The eventual price paid by the land agent was £10,000 but rather than be happy with £5,000 instead of the anticipated £250, the client wanted to know why the lawyer had agreed to such generous terms. Some people are just never satisfied.

Conversely, James once took on a Martello tower on the Sussex coast which the seller had bought for £50,000, quickly realised how much it would cost to convert and put it straight back on the private treaty market at the same price, where it had languished for eight months. James advised that we would achieve £100,000 but the owner insisted on a reserve of £50,000 to get rid of it. We had queues of cars at the viewings and the police arrived to control the traffic.

Three days before the sale we received a bid of £100,000 for a pre-auction exchange. The seller wanted to accept but James was sure it would make more. He was asked if he could guarantee a higher price to which, of course, the answer was 'no.' When the seller said he wanted certainty, James and the team were faced with daunting task of ringing hundreds of potential buyers to tell them it was sold prior.

After a quick chat, although I had not seen it, we agreed to underwrite the price at £100,000, meaning that if it sold for £90,000, we would be £10,000 out of pocket. James advised the client of our proposal but added that if it went for more than £100,000, we would be entitled to 50 per cent of the surplus, on the basis of no risk without reward. He did, however, stress that he would much prefer the seller to keep the lot in the auction and benefit fully from any surplus. This was confirmed in writing and a copy sent to the lawyer. The solicitor phoned the next day to seek my confirmation that if there was no bid and it remained unsold, we would pay the seller £100,000, to which the answer was how else could you interpret 'underwriting it at £100,000?'

The auction room was packed and the bidding finally finished at £265,000, our share of which was a staggering and somewhat embarrassing £82,500. I spoke to James from the rostrum and suggested that he should do a deal with the seller who, to his credit, would have none of it.

The conversation was on the lines of: 'James, you made me an extra £82,500 for which I am extremely grateful – I should have taken your advice, but a deal is a deal and no way will I expect a greater share.'

The lawyer wanted to know if we were intending to charge commission on the overage, and our accountant wanted to consider whether it was a commission or a trading profit.

Although a good result for both the seller and ourselves, we vowed that never again would we give a similar undertaking. We all felt quite uncomfortable about the result, despite the magnanimous comments by our client. Suffice it to say that our charitable donations that year were extremely generous.

I was on my mower one Saturday afternoon when a client stopped me to say that he had been offered an oast house just around the corner for £130,000. Without even seeing it I told him to buy it and put it straight into one of our auctions and he would make a handsome profit after fees and costs. I turned down his invitation to inspect it as my presence might make the sellers reconsider the price.

Within eight weeks we had sold the oast for £265,000, giving him a profit of 100 per cent less costs. The owner of the estate was not best pleased and sued his agents for the shortfall. I was asked to be an expert witness, the fee for which exceeded the commission and provided an interesting dialogue with the barrister in his chambers. There was no question of a backhander, it was more a case of the property having been on the market for three years and every time an offer was going ahead the seller withdrew. They just took their eye off the ball as the chances of proceeding to contracts was, in their opinion based on previous experience, highly unlikely. Not an excuse, but nonetheless an understandable reason.

We were asked to sell ten acres of woodland in Wrotham which our client had recently purchased but when we came to the inspection, could only make it five acres. I rang David, the auctioneer from Ward and Partners, and asked him how he came to make it ten acres. David was a man I admired greatly, a consummate professional, honest and showed his integrity when he confessed that his seller had told him it was ten acres. He had admitted that he had inspected it on a cold, wet Saturday afternoon and didn't check the measurements. I suggested that if the worst came to the worst to say that he used a 1/2500 scale instead of a 1/1250. It would produce the same result but sound better for the insurance claim, if there was one. We actually sold it for more than our seller paid and so the matter went no further. A salutary lesson which our appraisers are reminded of from time to time.

On the evening of a particularly busy auction day, I rang a regular buyer of mine to say that I had noticed he spent an inordinate amount of time signing the contracts at the clerk's desk – were we putting barriers in place to make the buying process less enjoyable? Firstly, Simon said he could not believe that with everything going on I would notice and secondly that it was his fault entirely, he did not expect to buy the lot, brought the wrong cheque book and dithered over which of his companies to nominate as the buyer. Apparently, our staff were amazingly patient and understanding and he had no complaints.

We have twice had a visit from the fire brigade to say that the saleroom was overcrowded and that the auction should be stopped. The first was in the Kensington Palace Hotel London, where I was selling for Stickley and Kent and the second at the Great Danes Hotel where 600 were in a room licensed to take just 350.

At the Kensington Palace Hotel I asked everyone not interested in the next twenty lots to leave and come back in thirty minutes - nobody moved! I then delayed the sale for an hour and the voyeurs gave up, leaving just the serious buyers to return to bid.

The fire officer at the Great Danes was a little more understanding and allowed the sale to continue 'on this one occasion,' as long as all the doors were left open, but that we should ensure it didn't happen again. Hence our move to the Clive Emson Conference Centre at the Kent Showground, where we sponsored a new building that had just been completed.

These are just a few of the many stories emanating from the 350,000 land and property lots I have sold under the hammer over the past fifty or so years. Perhaps I should write a book!

CHAPTER 13

A DECADE OF CORPORATE LUNCHES

The first five years following the launch of the business were a real struggle, having started at the beginning of the biggest recession in the property market since the war. When the fifteenth anniversary came around, we were well established and I thought it time to thank all the people who had been instrumental in our success.

It was agreed that we would hold a lunch for 300 to 350 at the Great Danes Hotel in Maidstone to include everyone who had supported us, from the boardmen, logo design studio, joint auctioneers, estate agents, lawyers, banks, accountants, architects, insurance brokers, printers, regular clients and buyers to friends and family. It was quite a list.

We soon realised that we were unique in being able to organise such an event, by that time being one of only two dedicated multi-lot property auctioneers in Kent, the other one being part of a chain of estate agents. Had any other profession tried to stage such an event they would have been reluctant to include their competitors or, indeed, reveal who their main clients were. Our company, on the other hand, was perceived as being a friendly business, complementing the services that other professionals could offer their clients without the risk of losing business to a competitor for other services such as retail sales, mortgages, managements etc. From day one our mantra was 'If it's for auction, it's for Emson – if not, then let a specialist deal with the situation.'

The guest list was carefully prepared, The Great Danes booked and the invitations sent out to coincide with anniversary of our launch date of October 1989. I was on my usual holiday in Spain during most of October when Hilary, our company secretary and director, phoned to say the there was a new general manager at the hotel and that the cost of the lunch would be the standard £30 a head plus wines and coffee – substantially more than I had envisaged.

I asked Hilary to arrange a meeting, preferably over lunch, with the new general manager and his events manager, Tracey, as soon as possible after my return to the UK. We had worked with Tracey for fifteen years and introduced a lot of business from the various charity events we had held at the hotel, plus seven regular auctions a year. As with all our suppliers, we thought of them as more like partners than a one-off customer.

When the meeting took place, the manager offered to buy us lunch and we chose from an à la carte menu priced at £16.50 a head. I queried how he could justify quoting us £30 a head for a set menu of 350 pre-sold lunches when the à la carte was nearly half that price? Surely, we should be able to benefit from the economies of scale and lack of wastage that must happen on a daily basis when the hotel didn't know in advance how many meals would be served?

The reply was not quite what I had expected.

'Mr Emson, it is what it is, I don't have to justify anything and anyway, haven't you already sent out the invitations?'

The look on Hilary and Tracey's faces was a memory I shall never forget.

I slowly removed a letter from my inside jacket pocket and said, 'Before the meeting I thought I would do a bit of research, and The Ashford International Hotel would be delighted to accommodate us, not only for the lunch but also our future auctions – it is fifteen miles down the motorway, and it would cost no more than a postage stamp to tell our guests of the change of venue, and the reason for that change.'

Time to start the conversation again. I was asked what figure a head I had in mind. Taking into account the cost of the à la carte, and that we only wanted soup as a starter, a main course of his choice but presumably chicken, plus a pudding, £15 seemed about right. I was told that the puddings alone were priced at £5.50 a head (probably Brake Brothers specials, which wholesaled at a fraction of the price).

After much discussion, we agreed to have a cheeseboard and a bottle of port on each table instead, which would be more acceptable to the guests for a lunch. When I go to this kind of event and see around 40 per cent of chocolate puddings left or just nibbled at, I don't regard it as a waste of food but rather a waste of £5.50 a head, which I would be paying! We eventually agreed on £20 a head to include reception drinks, half a bottle of house wine a head on the table and corkage for the port to complement the cheese.

Still, not a bad day for the hotel – Thursdays are not generally that busy for them anyway.

Michael Howard, the Member of Parliament for Folkestone and Hythe, agreed to be guest speaker. I had met Michael and Sandra on many occasions in the constituency and always found him a charming, dedicated and hard-working local MP. As a former QC, he made an amazing speech, taking the mickey out of me and giving the impression we were much closer friends that we actually were at the time. He did not request a fee, but I gave him one of the few solid silver gavels that I'd had made as a thank you. The last one I sold for the RICS charity, Lionheart, made £750.

The lunch went far better than we could have expected, much of which was due to Hilary's organisational skills and eye for detail. James and I had spent the previous Sunday afternoon working on the table plan, which proved quite a task as many of the invitees were not known to us personally but chosen by John and the other negotiators who knew the movers and shakers on their patch. We placed one member of staff as host for each of the thirty tables with the instruction to make sure each guest was given what they wanted, that their glasses were kept charged and to chat to anyone who seemed left out – as they would at a supper party in their own home.

The letter accompanying the invitation advised the guests to leave their cheque book and car at home and their diaries free for the afternoon; they were our guests and we would pick up the bill, including the free bar, as a thank you for supporting our business during the past fifteen years. They certainly took it literally, most not leaving until well after 5pm. The goodwill created by such a successful event is impossible to estimate, but in view of the wonderful letters and feedback, we decided it should become an annual event.

Over the next nine years the lunch became more and more popular and a must for most of the attendees. However, it never ceased to disappoint me that every year at least twenty people who accepted the invitation failed to attend; the 50 per cent who gave no apology either before or after were not troubled with another invitation. Twenty meals and two tables wasted, plus a waiting list for those who would have loved to join us. We all have times when unexpected business or illness prevent attending and a last-minute cancellation is inevitable, but no contact whatsoever is the height of rudeness. As always, anything that's free is usually undervalued.

For the next nine years we attracted some amazing speakers, including Digby Lord Jones (twice), Jeffrey Archer, John Gummer MP, Bob Marshall-Andrews, MP, the chief economist for HSBC, Dennis Turner (twice), Nigel Wheeler in his year as High Sheriff and, finally, the comedian Jethro who spoke at the 25th and last anniversary lunch. Each one of them was memorable for different reasons.

Digby Jones was Director General of the CBI when he first spoke to us. He was introduced to me by a former fellow member of the Round Table, Courtney, who actually followed me as Chairman of Table in 1984. He was a partner in a firm of chartered quantity surveyors in London when he first met Digby, one of the few speakers I have seen who can hold an audience spellbound for an hour with his enthusiasm and love of Great Britain and the positive spin on our economic future. He is the one who should have conducted the Brexit negotiations, he would have sorted it in no time.

I met Digby on many more occasions, either at events where he was speaking and also at a lunch I helped organise for Helen Grant, MP for Maidstone and the Weald, where he was guest speaker. He attended free of charge when he was Director General of the CBI and made only a modest charge for his time plus expenses when he came back to update us on the economy three years after his first appearance.

On his second appearance, I mentioned to him over lunch how our insurance company once paid a £3,500 claim for a sprained ankle made by someone who bought a balloon flight at a charity auction. It was of course an opportunist con; on landing, the claimant helped roll up the envelope and load it into the trailer and it was only three weeks later that the 'injury' manifested itself. The insurance company's view was that it was cheaper to pay the £3,500 than fight it out in court where the barrister's fees would eclipse the amount claimed. A commercial decision, but it grounded the charity flights for a year.

Digby was appalled and said that if I wished, I could auction a lunch with him in the House of Lords. If it didn't make

£500, buy it in – his time was worth more than that – and if we got to £750, then he would host two at the same time. We had four bidders fighting it out and when the price got to £2,500, I asked Digby, from the rostrum, 'If I buy the other two lunches, can you do all four?'

The answer was, of course, 'yes' and so we raised £10,000 for the local charities we support. What a result! I found out later that it was not the visit behind the scenes nor the lunch that made the money, it was exclusive time with Digby who was then the UK's overseas ambassador and each of the bidders was planning on setting up businesses abroad.

When I was president of the Old Roffensian Society, I decided to invite the headmaster of King's School to the annual lunch. John Gummer MP was an Old Boy and wrote a weekly column in the *Estates Gazette*, the property bible at the time, so I asked if he would care to be guest speaker at our property professionals' lunch. He is probably best remembered for feeding a burger to his daughter during the mad cow disease epidemic, but I thought his view on the property market would be of interest to my guests. The fee was agreed, but he said that he would have to leave by 2.30pm to get to a meeting in Birmingham. I said we could arrange a helicopter, which was declined. I hadn't realised he was an eco-friendly fanatic until he arrived in a Fiat Punto because it was economic on greenhouse gases. Oh dear, not quite the same as a helicopter then.

He asked one of the guests on top table what I drove, to which the answer was 'You don't want to know!' Then, as so often with MPs, once they get started it is impossible to stop them; he spoke for a good ninety minutes and left at 4pm. During his speech he berated local Government and planning officers. Paul Carter, leader of Kent County Council, was to follow Gummer, but instead of waiting to hear Paul's view he was off and away. It is not the first time I have witnessed MPs run before hearing the other point of view. It's probably why so many are out of touch with reality.

Another of our most enjoyable and witty speakers was the Labour MP for Medway, Bob Marshall-Andrews QC, a self-effacing orator with such wonderful stories. He arrived by train and walked the 1.5 miles from Hollingbourne Station to the hotel, despite being offered a lift. We chatted over lunch and he observed that there must be some guests we would prefer not to invite but were duty bound to do so. Of course he was right, there were one or two. I told him that we put them on Table 1 and then they would strut around the reception with the sense of misplaced self-importance that had made them candidates for the list in the first place. When they entered the main dining hall, Table 1 would be out of the way in one of the far corners – miles from the top table, preferably near the kitchen doors.

How embarrassed was I when Bob stood up and his first words were 'Tell me – where is Table 1?' He let me off lightly, but displayed all the qualities of an experienced barrister. When discussing whether there was a budget for the speaker's fee, he asked what Gummer had got paid – £1,500 to his company account, I replied. That would be fine for him then, but could we pay £750 to a UK charity and £750 to an overseas aid charity? The difference between a Labour MP and a Conservative MP, I told myself.

I heard from one or two sources that guests were uncomfortable taking our hospitality on such a regular basis and could they not pay for their tickets? This would, however, have taken away our ability to invite those we actually wanted there. After the second lunch, we made it known that we would hold a charity raffle so that those who wished to acknowledge the hospitality could buy tickets. It proved a good compromise and raised around £7,000 for Young Lives Foundation, The Taverners and Playing for Success, all of which were charities close to my heart.

One year I was popping out to spend around £500 on raffle prizes when I thought, what a waste of money, most of the attendees would buy a bottle of champagne or whisky if they wanted one. Instead, I announced that there would be a raffle as usual but this time it would be with a difference: there were no prizes, so everyone would be equally disappointed. The tickets were still £20 each or three for £50. That raffle raised £7,500, every penny of which went to the charities, who shared £2,500 each.

After the auction I received a rather pompous letter from one of the Medway solicitors in attendance pointing out that it was illegal to offer discount rates in a raffle as it altered the odds unfairly. I think anyone selling raffle tickets would be aware of this, but in a charity setting a police raid would be highly unlikely. I did of course, remind him that as there were no prizes, just who was being disadvantaged?

Jeffrey Archer was a close friend of my brother and I had met him on a couple of occasions. I thought I would ask him to be guest speaker; with a room full of perceived crooks, why not get the one who had actually done time in Her Majesty's prison? He is also an outstanding speaker and competent charity auctioneer. When I asked him if he would be guest speaker, he suggested a fee of £7,500 – well above my budget – so I said if we get nearer the time and he had an empty diary, might £1,500 be attractive for a lunch engagement? He came back straight away and confirmed that would be fine.

He couldn't believe the guests on his table, one of whom was John Sunley, a prominent, larger-than- life Kent businessman who was also well-respected in London circles. John was a friend of mine following a few purchases from the auction; always trustworthy and true to his word. Looking at the place cards on my table, Jeffrey asked me with some incredulity whether it was THE John Sunley, wondering what he would be doing at a little provincial lunch.

'I'm not sure,' I said, adopting the stance of a small-time country auctioneer with a straw behind his ear. 'he's the one I know and shoot with on his country estate at Godmersham, does he go to London as well?'

Jeffrey delivered his standard speech, which I had heard so many times. He did, however, thank me publicly for not mentioning a certain four years in his career when introducing him. Although it would have been good for a cheap laugh, he was my guest and shown the respect that any guest should receive.

The chief economist for HSBC, Dennis Turner, shared his thoughts at two of our lunches – a man with the most amazing energy and interesting facts peppered with anecdotes such as 'my wife always keeps within her budget – even if she has to borrow to do so!' Sadly, he died too young but probably lived at twice the rate of most.

Grace at the majority of lunches was delivered by Canon Norman Woods, the vicar of Hythe for twenty-five years, a good friend of mine and always guaranteed to give a well-proportioned, fresh, humorous but dignified grace, a true talent. He was sitting next to Michael Howard and was surprised to hear that Michael's son was an evangelical Christian and asked with some incredulity if he really believed every aspect of the stories in the Bible, even Adam and Eve? 'Yes,' replied Michael somewhat diffidently. 'Well, he needs a good talking to' was the response. End of conversation.

For the twenty-fifthth anniversary we really pushed the boat out, holding a lunch for 550 at the Clive Emson Conference Centre at the Kent Showground, where we had held our property auctions for some years. The guest list was extensive, but sadly a few mistakes were made with the list which only came to light when James and I were working on the table plan. Some agents and friends I had known for forty years or more were missed out or put in the wrong section.

Andrew, who I once worked with and had been a loyal introducer, Paul, who ran a successful estate agency in Saltwood, Steve, the former MD of a construction company with whom I played golf and shared an interest in clocks were, for reasons which I still do not understand, all overlooked. Rather in the same vein as the property auctions, I focus on the ones who slipped through the net rather than revel in the glory of those that did well. Three or four people out of 550 might seem a small error, but it still rankles to this day, despite each one of them being more than understanding – which almost made it worse. They must have been very hurt when others in the profession were talking about the forthcoming lunch of the year to which they had been invited for the past nine.

For this special lunch I decided to ask the comedian Jethro to be guest speaker on the basis that we had taken auctions to Cornwall so he could bring a bit of Cornwall to Kent. We had tried to get him before but without success. Luckily, Katy from our West Country Office knew him personally through family connections and the booking was confirmed. Again, it's not what you know…

The guest list comprised the great and good of Kent, including Deans, Deputy Lieutenants, former and current High Sheriffs, Members of Parliament, senior Council leaders and many of the most successful businessmen and women in the county, all of whom I knew personally through the various charities, clubs and organisations to which I belong - together with, of course the hundreds of clients and contacts made through the business over twenty-five years.

We had displays by those we had sponsored, among them a dressage rider, a gold medal gymnast and of course the hot air balloon. It was a windy day on high ground and we had trouble tethering the balloon, even with three Range Rovers as static weights. I cannot tell you how many commented that the balloon was obviously ours as it was full of hot air and even then, we couldn't keep it up for long! Rather set the tone for the day.

Jethro's manager made all sorts of requests. He needed a private room with a sofa and hot and cold drinks. Jethro did not want to join us for lunch as he didn't eat before a performance. The stage had to be rearranged, despite the fact that all he had was a stool and microphone, the PA system wasn't good enough – a comedian will go flat if the audience can't hear the punchline. I did mention that we had Mark, our own sound recordist who attended all auctions in the same building and that just like comedians, auctioneers don't work too well if people can't hear them.

The manager did a sound test, came over to the console and twiddled a few of the knobs then went back to try again, remarking 'so much better!' When he was out of earshot, Mark said, 'Funny, that console isn't even connected to the microphone on the stage!' When shown the rest room, Jethro said it was quite unnecessary as he wanted to wander about and in fact took a great interest in the dressage as he was a respected judge at horse shows in Cornwall.

When we sent out the invitations, I did mention that Jethro's jokes were not always politically correct and contained some bad language. What an understatement! From the minute he started there was a mixture of hilarious laughter and stark amazement. I could see some of the audience looking at many of the dignitaries to gauge their reaction; some were laughing, others not so much. As Amanda, a lovely and dignified lady, said to me afterwards, 'Some of the stories were amusing, but I am wondering in what environment I could repeat them.'

Sometime later, when having lunch with Norman, I mentioned that the choice of speaker, on reflection, may have been a mistake.

'May have been a mistake?' exclaimed the very Reverend Canon, 'May have been a mistake? It was definitely one of the biggest mistakes you have made in your life, dear boy!' Oh, if only he knew.

Probably around 80 per cent of the audience loved Jethro's humour and were heard repeating the stories for months to come. It is of course the 20 per cent that I dwell on – no guest should ever be embarrassed. Just shows, you can't please all of the people all of the time. However, in hindsight, Digby Jones or Bob Marshall-Andrews would definitely have been a safer choice.

It was an expensive promotion as the usual rules applied: leave your cheque book and car at home, the party is on us. We also gave each guest a party bag to leave with which contained branded pens, pencils and other merchandise and even a specially engraved miniature gavel paper weight. It did, however, mark a fabulous quarter of a century in business.

The 25th anniversary lunch also represented the end of an era. The business had by now expanded from Essex to the West Country and it was unreasonable to expect our many friends and clients from further afield to travel to Kent for a lunch, so the decision was made by James that in future we would host a smaller event of 80 to 100 in each region to ensure that all those who supported us were accommodated, without Dad's mates muscling in on another freebie!

CHAPTER 14

MENTORING YOUNG PEOPLE

When I attended a routine Maidstone Rotary Club lunch meeting in 1998, I had no way of knowing just how much it would affect my life. The guest speaker was a lady from the YMCA who came to ask for a donation of £100 to buy stationery for the local Homework Club.

This was a forum for underprivileged children, mainly from two council estates where 25 per cent of children were in single-parent homes, 50 per cent of families had no wage earner and received clothing and food grants and there was a general prevalence of poor parenting skills and a high level of illiteracy among parents. Poverty was a real issue, with incomes around 60 per cent of the minimum wage. It was a real eye opener for many of the Rotarians.

Not only did they need funds but also volunteers to help out at the Homework Club, where children in the 11-16 age range would come after school. Most were in homes where either schoolwork was frowned upon or the parents were just ill-equipped to help their young ones. That meant every morning the children would start badly, with no homework to hand in and a black mark against them. The speaker cautioned that the children were often difficult and might even smell, due to a lack of personal hygiene.

She finished by saying that any volunteering assistance for just a couple of hours a week would be welcome. I have always had a good rapport with young people, possibly the reason why Becky and James' friends always loved coming to our house, so I agreed to participate. I also donated enough paper and pens to keep them going for a very long time indeed.

The meetings were held in a church hall in the middle of the Shepway Estate in Maidstone. On the first meeting the social worker told me that it was the tea and toast that got the kids to the club. The format was a group chat and chill time, followed by games in the big hall and then homework. Sometimes we would walk to the nearby library to show the youngsters how to choose suitable books and look after them until they were returned in good condition.

I have to say that it was a welcome change from the pressures of business. What I like about young people is their honesty, a trait sadly failing among many adults when in a property buying and selling environment – even the most honest and genuine people sometimes have no conscience in lying when engaged in a property transaction.

I also found the repartee quite refreshing and enlightening. On one visit I arrived, as usual, in the white Saab convertible. Eleven-year-old Gary commented, 'Nice motor, Cloive,' to which I replied if he worked hard, then he too could have a nice car one day. The look on his face was a picture.

'Work hard? Dad don't work, uncle don't work, Mum don't work, so why should I?'

'But they won't have nice cars,' I suggested.

'If they want one, they'll nick it,' was the response. 'But don't worry, I'll put the word out and nobody will touch yours.' I felt a sense of relief being protected by an eleven-year-old boy.

One week he arrived at homework club with a shaven head. 'God – who did your hair?' I asked.

'Why?'

'So I never go there.'

Gary told me that he had been in court that morning.

'But they don't shave your head, surely?'

With a frustrated sigh he explained that the old women 'what he mugged' was looking for a small boy with long hair and so didn't identify him as her mugger and he got off.

Gary was a bright boy with so much potential. When we were working on some maths, I congratulated him on a good job well done and from the look on his face, it was obvious that he was not used to any praise whatsoever. The smile said it all. A bit of encouragement went a long way and motivated him to produce more excellent results. I have always believed that a carrot is better than a stick.

His sister Serena, some three years older, also attended the club and we got on really well, mainly because I treated her with respect. She would write poems for me that were so talented, if only the skill could be channelled. I think she appreciated my non-judgemental approach and openness. Again, she was a bright child so I was shocked when the social worker said she would probably be pregnant before she was fifteen. A completely different life and one that I had no idea existed until getting involved at the coalface.

I helped at the club for three years, joining the group for a couple of hours on a Thursday afternoon. I got to know many of the children quite well, though it does of course take time to gain their confidence; most are used to the 'suits' – here today, gone tomorrow. When stimulated and spoken to rather than at, most children are receptive – as long as tea and toast is on the menu.

The problem with the Homework Club was that if a child was excluded from school, then there would be no homework and they couldn't attend. The attendees were also quite transient; almost as soon as you got to know them and gained their trust, they would be off for a variety of reasons. These could range from peer pressure (it wasn't cool to study) to permanent exclusion from school and, more often than not, that the family had been evicted and moved out of the area or a parent had been imprisoned, leading to a care order for the children.

I mentioned my frustration at building trust over a number of weeks then to never see the young person again to one of the social workers, who suggested that maybe becoming an Independent Visitor with Church In Society might be a more suitable role for me. I was put in touch with Adrian, which started me out on a completely different journey.

The training for this newly created role took place over the course of three consecutive Saturdays at the rather spartan office of the Church In Society children's division in Marsham Street, Maidstone. Meetings were headed up by Adrian and ably assisted by Stephen, two people whom I got to know well over the next decade or two.

The training was as much about our safety as that of the young person with whom we were paired. Every child in care wants nothing more than to be loved and to be part of a family. There is a difficult balance of gaining trust but not letting them get too close and create expectations that cannot be fulfilled. We learned that the Independent Visitor would be the only person in that child's life who was not actually paid to be there and that most of the children had no contact with their birth family. They were literally alone in a world of rules and regulations, whether at school or in a care home.

At first I didn't realise what a very special role I was about to play and one that we all agreed to sign up to for a minimum of three years. We were told one of the reasons children in care have such a lack of self-confidence is that in most cases foster homes, social workers and schools change with monotonous regularity, creating absolutely no feelings of belonging or security. It sounded a bit far-fetched to me back then, but it was the main reason for the three-year commitment.

The role is one of complete trust. It is one of the very rare occasions where a child and adult are alone, one to one, whether driving in the car, walking, bowling, cinema or swimming but never at the IV's home. It is also where the young person can speak openly to the IV with the promise that whatever is said will go no further, unless the young person wants it to or if the IV has a concern about the child's safety. The importance of this cannot be overestimated in a culture where a report is made on every child, every day, on their behaviour, hygiene, etc. That report forms part of a review held every six months and attended by the chairman, social worker, care home or foster parent, school liaison officer and, if requested by the young person, their Independent Visitor to speak on their behalf.

Soon after completion of the mandatory enhanced police check, I was introduced to Daz in a children's care home in Deal. I will never forget the setting. This little mite was brought into the room and told to sit on an upright chair opposite three adults, also on upright chairs, two of whom he had never met before, to establish whether he and I would be likely to get on. After the first interview either party can say if they are not happy with the arrangement.

Daz, who was dressed in a blue oversized football shirt and shorts that were also too big, looked confused. We chatted for about half an hour trying to find common ground. Did he like cars? No. Sport? No. School? No. Animals? No. Reading? No. Television? Sometimes. A glimmer of hope to work on, although I watched very little, if any, TV. He appeared scared and with no self-confidence whatsoever. It was a real challenge for me, as I can usually find at least one subject to develop with anyone I meet. He told me later that he was not sure why he was being asked to talk to a fat, bald-headed old man anyway – which goes to show that he'd found his tongue after all.

The concept of the IV mentoring is that about twice a month the two do an activity that all the other children in the house are not part of – a sort of quasi-grandparental role. The main thing is to listen and to give advice when requested, but without being judgemental. On the first outing he decided it would be nice to go to the Whitstable wave pool, which suited me as I also enjoy swimming. I picked him up and tried chatting on the way. I asked his opinion on something to get him chatting and he told me, quite matter-of-factly, that no one bothered about his opinion and why would they? Absolutely no self-worth or sense of confidence – a product of being in the care system since he was three months old.

When we arrived the centre was closed, but Daz took the disappointment well, almost as if he didn't care and later explained that he was used to being let down at the last minute. I have found that most children in care are reluctant to show emotion to anyone and are non-materialistic. If they show any affection towards something it will be used as a tool to enforce discipline; if they don't show interest in anything, then it is less likely to be taken away.

What gets most eleven-year-old boys laughing is a good lavatorial joke – totally inappropriate (a word I would hear with some frequency), of course. I told him a joke that got him rocking in his seat. Up until then he was having trouble placing me in a box; social worker, psychologist, do-gooder

– at this point he gave up as he had never met anyone like me before.

'Tell me again, Clive,' he asked.

'Well, actually Daz, a joke doesn't work too well the second time round.'

'Go on, tell me,' he insisted so I told him the same joke again, which resulted in the same mirth. 'Tell me again,' he said.

'The third time won't work Daz, why do you want me to say it again?'

Shock horror, he wanted to tell the others when he got back to the house. I could hear myself saying,' You mustn't tell the others, it's a secret between the two of us – no, not a secret (training said we mustn't have secrets). 'This was going to be a challenge alright.

After we had met a few times, the problem was not getting Daz to talk, but keeping him quiet! He became more and more relaxed when we met and for the first time in his life, he had found someone he could not only trust implicitly but who also wasn't going to walk away. The very essence of the IV programme, which is a statutory requirement for all young people in care who want one.

We had our moments and it was a steep learning curve, more for me than him. The first time that I felt I was really making a difference was within the first three months of being paired. Daz bit a care worker, who restrained him by holding his arms close to his body after he had kicked off. The police were called and Daz was arrested and taken to the local police station, handcuffed in the back of a squad car. The date for the hearing in the Magistrates Court was set and I asked if Daz wanted me there. The care home manager was in an invidious position; he had to support his colleague and Daz was left to the mercy of a duty solicitor, who told him that they had photographs, he was guilty, so admit it and move on.

I suggested that we plead not guilty but was advised that all staff who had witnessed the event and fellow residents would then be brought in to give evidence, after which he would go back to face them at the home. I asked to speak on behalf of the defendant and as the bench had never heard of an Independent Visitor, it was agreed that I could appear as his mentor. I explained to the court that Daz was not there because he bit a care worker, but because he was in care. If every child that bit a sibling or parent was dragged before a court, they would need to sit until midnight every day.

I pleaded for a conditional discharge but as there was no doubt that he had bitten the care worker, this was not an option, so he was given the lightest sentence possible: a three-month supervision order. If only I knew what effect that would have on him in later life, I would have fought his case much harder, but probably with the same outcome.

Daz introduced me to McDonald's in Ramsgate. When we entered, I looked at the menu board and failed to identify anything that actually represented a meal. Daz took over, explained the process and ordered something for both of us – he was now in charge for the first time in his life. No tablecloths I could accept, but no knives and forks? The whole experience was well out of my comfort zone, but I was there for him and not him for me.

Little did I realise that within two years I would be thrown out of the very same establishment. One afternoon when I met Daz after school he asked if his mate Marcus could join us. If that's what he wanted I could see no reason why not, especially as Marcus was also in care, albeit in another home. It's quite natural for young teenagers to want to test the boundaries and try to shock the adult. Marcus told me that he had a condom and did I want to see it? My answer was that I did know what a condom looked like but was glad he had one in order to avoid further candidates for care in a few years' time. Not the answer he was expecting, so he removed it from his pocket, luckily still in its dog-eared original wrapper. It tastes of raspberries, he said, just before taking a mouthful of coke. 'Amazing,' I said, 'I didn't realise that girls had taste glands down there,' which resulted in a guffaw and coke being sprayed all over our table and a few others around us. The manager came over and said that if we wished to leave, he would not object.

'Are we being thrown out?' I asked, to which the reply was 'Yes, I suppose so.' I was about to say that I had been asked to leave worse places than McDonald's in Ramsgate but not even I could stretch the truth that far.

The original house that accommodated Daz and eleven other looked-after children had an unusual way of dealing with residents. If one of them looked as if they were about to kick off – and believe me, they had much reason to lose it – rather than be talked down, they would be goaded so that the inevitable commotion that followed could be dealt with at a time that would suit the staff rather than wait for an incident over the meal table or bedtime.

During this period the thinking was to put looked-after children in smaller homes with just two or three others in order to replicate a family situation. Daz was moved to Ramsgate, where Lille was the person in charge. Daz was struggling with his homework and as he was the only resident at the time, I suggested that Lille might help him. I was told quite firmly that was not her remit. Some family environment! She was one of the most depressing and unmotivated people I have ever met, totally unsuited to the job, quite content to sit on her backside watching television rather than helping those in her charge. We had a number of run-ins, two of which are worth mentioning.

For Daz's fifteenth birthday I got clearance to buy him a bike to give him a bit more freedom. The bike was delivered, a very special gift. When I visited him ten days later, the bike was still in the hall, having not been ridden. Apparently, he was not allowed to ride the bike as he didn't have a helmet, so we went into town and bought one for £10. The next time I visited it was still in the same place. This time he was not allowed to take it out because he didn't have a proficiency test certificate. Three weeks walking past a present he was prevented from using; would any parent treat a child in the same way?

Eventually the bike was stored in an outside locked shed in an enclosed rear garden surrounded by a six-foot wall in the centre of a row of terraced houses. We were then told that it had been stolen from the shed. There was a crime number and I suggested that the insurance should cover a replacement. After four weeks and nothing I told Lille that I would talk directly to the head office, only to be informed that a claim had not been made as it was under £100. Lies and disloyalty are two traits that I have real difficulty with. When eventually a new bike was bought, Lille suggested that it should be his Christmas present. No, I insisted, it was his birthday present. Jealousy is another characteristic I struggle with.

The atmosphere in the house was toxic and when Daz left school at sixteen he was leaving the house early and returning late, at which point a row would erupt. Every day he would leave a little earlier and return a little later. I established that he was spending the day in a tower block with friends where drugs were an issue. I don't think Daz was into drugs himself, but it was only a matter of time. I was concerned and having discussed it with Sue, we decided to suggest that he could stay with us at Bitford for a couple of weeks if a respite home could not be found. This would give time for tempers on both sides to calm down.

The reply from Tower Hamlets, the local authority responsible for Daz, was that it was inappropriate for a looked-after child to stay with an IV, even though Sue and I had both been police checked. I knew what I was doing when I sent an email saying that it was good to have on record that social services thought it more appropriate for a vulnerable young man to be in a known drugs environment rather than be removed to a place of safety. As is so often the way in any large organisation, the person at the top is protected from news which could reflect badly on the middle and lower management.

The head of Tower Hamlets Social Services, whom I had tried to contact many times before, asked for a meeting to discuss the situation. We met at the Young Lives Foundation office in Maidstone. I cannot tell you how many times since I met Daz that the rule book was thrust in my face. For example, I was told it was against the rules for him to drive my car in my four-acre field, something that most teenagers enjoy. When I asked for a copy of the rule book and how comprehensive it must be to cover driving cars on private land, she said that there was no such publication and what was wrong with driving the car under supervision anyway? The assistant care home manager piped up that he could imagine Daz sitting on my lap in the car, which I thought said rather more about him than me. Plus the fact that with the size of my stomach it would be a physical impossibility anyway. It was also agreed that there is little danger in a four-acre field and any damage would be down to me as it was my car and my field. I think the meeting was an eye-opener for all of us. The outcome was that Daz was moved from Lille's care: result.

The pastoral care at Daz's secondary mainstream Catholic school in Dover was exceptional. As with most looked-after children, the academic results were not good, but at least he was not excluded and benefited from a daily routine and discipline. Sister Carmel was his mentor, a gentle, caring nun who kept in touch with Daz and me long after he left.

After Daz left school, he needed more help than ever as there was little prospect of meaningful employment with few academic qualifications, no transport and a less-than-enthusiastic attitude towards a working environment. After some discussion, he thought it might be a good plan to do overseas aid work, so we started the process. After completing umpteen forms and attending two meetings in London, Daz was finally accepted for a placement in the United States. Then came the shock; because he had a criminal record dating from the assault when he was eleven, he was refused a visa. Yet another kick in the teeth, which he accepted in the same resigned manner as he'd displayed when the swimming bath was closed.

Although the original arrangement was for three years, Daz and my family have kept in close contact. When he married Kim, Sue and I flew back from Spain to join Becky, Steve and my granddaughter Livvy at the ceremony and we were the only people on his side of the church. It is almost unimaginable what it must be like to have no family and few friends. The care system doesn't engender close relationships, which stems from the insecurity of constantly being moved and let down by the very people paid to be there for you.

One of the services offered by YLF is sending mentors into schools where a student has dropped several places in a short time. Clearly the youngsters cannot talk either to their teachers or parents, otherwise the situation would not have arisen. I was asked to mentor three such students. The meetings are held at their school for half an hour once a week for up to three months. My first candidate was a young man of thirteen. One has to tread carefully as the perception of mum and dad, a sibling or two and a dog or cat sitting around a cosy fire is the exception rather than the norm.

Anyway, we established during the second meeting that Connor in fact came from a close family and that six months earlier his grandmother had died, just about the time when his work started deteriorating. He said that he had been very close to Granny and he thought everyone else in the family was too, but when she died they had a big party to celebrate her death and were all drinking and laughing. I did suggest that when he was at the church, he would have seen how sad they were and that the wake was to celebrate her life and the love that she'd brought everyone.

Apparently, his parents had decided that he would be too upset to attend the funeral and so he stayed at home. So many parents make the same mistake. Children are much more resilient than adults give them credit for and they miss a really important part of the grieving process, or is it perhaps that parents don't want to be seen as emotionally vulnerable by their offspring? Once Connor had appreciated the situation, he was back in the top group again. Job done.

Dillan was much more complex. He and his two siblings had recently been taken into care. His sister was sixteen, Dillan fourteen and Ryan just twelve. They were all at the same academy and had been summoned to the headteacher's office after school. They waited in silence for an hour, not knowing why they had been detained, until a social worker arrived to tell them that at a court hearing earlier in the day social services had been given a full custody order over all three. Ryan was sent to Sevenoaks, Dillan to Ashford and his sister remained in Maidstone. Their whole life turned upside down, not only parted from their parents but also each other. The court gave sanction because the mother and father had poor parenting skills and the house was deemed unhygienic and unsuitable for the children. Surely it would have been kinder and a lot cheaper to provide a cleaning service but that, it seems, is not an option. Perhaps if the authorities had to pay for their decisions it might become a tool in the box. Amazing how much money can be spent when it is not your own and the taxpayer is picking up the bill.

I reported back that Dillan would need more mentoring than a three-month, half-hour session and so he became my second charge as an Independent Visitor. The main problem was that Dillan was prone to running away, as was his brother Ryan when he was a bit older. Dillan was not an easy placement for a foster carer. Understandably, he didn't want to be there; his life had been turned on its head and all he wanted was to mix with his mates rather than be lodged twenty miles away. In the next year he was moved three times, attended two schools and had four social workers. He was not allowed to see his parents, even under supervision, and meetings with his siblings were not encouraged because of his attitude.

After 18 months the third six-month review meeting was arranged. I asked if he would like me to attend and was told I could if I liked. I said that I was rather hoping for a reply to the effect 'Thank you Clive for offering to give up your time' or 'No thanks, I will be fine.' He explained that it would be as big a waste of time as the previous two, everyone would gather round a table and make decisions that would never be adopted but they would have ticked another box. To me this was a real eye-opener, for someone so young to be so perceptive and see it for what it really was. It was agreed that I would attend.

Part way through the meeting the chairman said, 'Dillan, it is difficult to come to a decision with which you will be happy if you constantly say "whatever" to everything.'

I said that I thought I could help here and repeated Dillan's view that no decision would be implemented as no time scales had been placed on anything we had discussed and just how could it make sense to find a new foster placement before establishing which school would take him?

The chairman latched on to this immediately and asked the social worker for time scales and a logical implementation of the plans agreed. One thing that makes review meetings difficult is the process of asking if the young person has any complaints about their accommodation, school or social worker when all three representatives concerned are sitting at the same table.

Running away was a constant concern of mine. A fifteen-year-old boy roaming the streets late at night is asking for trouble, so I lent him a mobile phone and told him to call me to say he was safe. I didn't need to know where he was because I would have to pass that on to the police, and they have enough to do without looking for errant juveniles. The authorities eventually moved Dillan to Bexleyheath in a house run by two police officers, where he was fostered until he was eighteen. It was ideal – nowhere for him to run to and reasonable but enforced parameters. They were also very protective of him.

Dillan has always been a hard worker. He would get up at 5am to catch a bus and walk to Bluewater, where he was employed by Jack Wills. He had a job at a Turkish restaurant as a waiter and after three weeks was told he was only on probation; they didn't need him anymore and that he would not be paid for the hours he had put in. The police lady foster carer popped in to the restaurant in uniform and suggested that they either paid him or expect a raid at an inconvenient time. Dillan was paid in full – in cash.

When a looked-after child reaches eighteen, they are no longer in the care system. They lose their social worker and foster home and are moved to semi-independent living accommodation or bed and breakfast emergency housing. With both Dillan and Daz there were no plans until the very last minute. They had in mind moving Daz back to Tower

Hamlets on his eighteenth birthday, somewhere he hadn't lived since he was eight, while with Dillan the plan was to move him into a room in a house of multiple occupation on the very estate he had been removed from when he was fourteen and just two houses away from where his parents still lived.

Helen Grant MP arranged for me to see the Children's Minister at the House of Commons to explain that the 'stay put' legislation was not working. The initiative allowed the young person to stay with their foster carers if they wished and the carer would receive payment to avoid a move. What the legislation did not take into account was the fact that the income of around £500 a week for full care would be reduced to £68 for letting a room at the housing benefit rate. Not only would the carer lose £430 a week but they would have to declare to their insurers that they were now taking in a lodger. As is so often the way with Government, the phrase 'stay put' was a good sound bite, but in reality, was just not viable in the majority of cases.

There are enough stories regarding the trials and tribulations of being an Independent Visitor over a fifteen-year period to fill a book by itself. On reflection, I have really enjoyed my time with both lads and still see them. Daz is in full-time employment and living in Folkestone, Dillan has a long-term girlfriend and a baby son and daughter. Both are hard workers and contribute to society, and both still call me when they have a problem. So much for a three-year agreement.

CHAPTER 15

THE YOUNG LIVES FOUNDATION

I had been an independent visitor to Darren under the Church in Societies Kent Independent Visitors (KIVS) banner for about three years when Adrian, the chap in charge, asked me to pop in to see him. My immediate thought was that I had done something against the rules, yet again. How wrong I was.

Adrian explained that he was becoming increasingly frustrated at the length of time it took to get a decision from the diocese on mundane matters and had agreed with them, in principle, to take over the children's section and form a new charity, which he would call the Young Lives Foundation.

He asked if I would not only be a trustee but also chairman of the new board. I'd never been a trustee before and couldn't have imagined how it would change my life. I said I'd be delighted to chair the board as long as every trustee brought something to the table - and that there should be no more than five to begin with.

I had seen many charities where some of the trustees were only there to be a name on the paper, so I told Adrian, 'If they want to come just to get on the Honours List, tell them to go elsewhere.' What a hypocrite I felt fifteen years later.

He had already approached another independent visitor, Russell, a Deputy Lieutenant, which left two more to join plus, of course, Adrian who would attend all the meetings as CEO.

On a skiing holiday I persuaded a good friend of mine I knew from the Maidstone Club Committee, the senior partner in Maidstone's largest law firm, to become a founder trustee. It's always important to have somebody with a knowledge of the law on board and, furthermore, Geoff had worked with schools and young people in the courts and was also a director of an investment business, so had a good handle on finances.

I felt it was equally vital to have somebody else in the team who would not only have a good rapport with children, but also had experience in building a business from scratch. My friend Jo, who has amazing energy, an ability to communicate at all levels and whose opinion I respect, succumbed to my plea that we needed her with us.

The team was in place and at the first meeting it was agreed that my firm's chartered accountants would be the auditors and that our bank would handle the account.

All staff working for the children's side of the church were transferred across to YLF, including Adrian's assistant Stephen and Jenny, who understood the accounts and had been with the team for a number of years.

With all our ducks in a row, Young Lives Foundation was formed and ready for business. While there was great enthusiasm, clearly the charity needed funds to supplement the grants for statutory services paid for by Kent County Council and Medway Council.

I once shared an office with Paul Carter, who was in property and we had a mutual liking for cars (he rallied a vintage Bentley at the time). Later, as leader of KCC, he was happy to come to the seminar we arranged on YLF's first anniversary. I will never forget Paul's comment that when he asked his secretary to brief him on the charity, all she could find out was that Clive was involved!

During the first twelve months Adrian and I were getting to know each other from a different perspective and cracks were beginning to show. I was constantly told that the ethos of a charity differs greatly from that of a business. Adrian seemed quite content to carry on as before with no real ambition to expand the charity and provide a service to a greater number of vulnerable children. He was in his comfort zone and therefore content.

I saw my role as filling the gaps where Adrian was lacking experience; having worked for large organisations all his life, raising funds seemed abhorrent to him, but I knew it was vital in order to reduce our dependency on government grants. Brand awareness was also alien to him. He didn't appreciate that if people don't know who you are and what you do, they will never come to you.

I was at the time president of Playing for Success, a fabulous charity that took struggling young students after school to play football with Thanet and Ebbsfleet, cricket with Kent and go-karting at Rochester. The youngsters would meet their idols, then do their homework and the next morning at school would not only be ahead of the game academically but also, for a change, the envy of their peers.

Sadly, as this was not a statutory requirement, when government cutbacks were brought in funding was pulled overnight, leaving the staff without jobs and the students struggling once again. That was something that I didn't want to happen to YLF on my watch.

I asked Heather, a friend of mine from Becky's school days and a professional fundraiser, if she could help. She loved the charity so much she agreed to work *pro bono* but her first meeting with Adrian, which I attended, was embarrassing. He was downright rude and questioned everything that she proposed – suggesting that he knew better, but proving beyond doubt that he really didn't understand the whole concept. And why should he? He had never needed to bother with fundraising before.

After the meeting Heather wanted to walk away, but we needed her so I persuaded her to agree that Stephen and I would be the conduit with Heather and that Adrian would take a back seat. This didn't sit comfortably with Adrian as he wanted to control everything; however, he soon realised it was non-negotiable.

One of the first initiatives I introduced was a barbecue held at Bitford for Independent Visitors and their young people. It was a perfect event for the volunteers to show that they were not alone and a relaxed and enjoyable way to show off their charges. It was also one of the rare occasions when, apart from not peeing in the pool, there were no rules. Stephen knew every volunteer, every child (all eighty of them) and their histories. To him it was not a job but a vocation. Ice cream George attended every year with his vintage tricycle dispensing copious cornets – the record for any one child was seventeen. When George died, he bequeathed his tricycle to me so that the tradition could continue, which it has to this day.

Every year King's School Canterbury held their leaver's ball in a massive marquee on the Godmersham Estate, courtesy of Fiona Sunley. Heather approached them both to ask if YLF could use the marquee for a fundraising event the night before on the understanding that everything would be left as we found it by 8am the following morning.

It was an amazing opportunity for YLF, and King's School liked the fact that less-privileged children would benefit from their facilities. Adrian decided that he would take charge of ticket sales and promotion of the event. Just three weeks before the evening, he mentioned that they had only sold fifteen tickets so would cancel the summer supper. My response was quite firm. 'I will take it from here.' I emailed all my friends and contacts and we managed to fill 200 seats within a week. Since then, the supper has become my baby and an annual event which has raised around £50,000 in unrestricted funds.

One of the problems we had was that the trustees were considered by Adrian to be no more than a governance requirement imposed on him by the Charity Commission. We met every two months and it was a constant irritation that recommendations made by the trustees were not acted upon, as it was deemed the management's decision whether or not to do so.

The final straw came when we lost a substantial contract with KCC and the board was not advised for eight weeks. The feedback was that the contract was in the bag until the presentation by our CEO to the providers who were told, rather condescendingly, that they really didn't know what they were talking about and should rewrite the requirements.

The board, and especially Geoff, lost confidence and it was my job to retrieve the situation. Luckily, Adrian must have realised that he was in an untenable position and before I could say anything at the meeting that I had convened to address the matter, he started by telling me that he had decided he wanted to retire to the West Country. His resignation was accepted and so a new CEO had to be found.

I will, however, be forever grateful to Adrian for his vision in laying the foundations for YLF. I am sure that had it remained as part of Church in Society, the services offered would not reflect the vital role that the charity plays today in making a difference to so many young people in Kent.

In my mind, there was no better person to take the helm than Stephen; he was young, enthusiastic and in my view had probably been holding it together for some time. At first he was not sure if he was up to the job, but after assurances that he would have the full backing of the board and we would provide cover for tasks outside his comfort zone, he stepped up to the plate. In my view that was probably the best decision I ever made and the real turning point for the charity.

I continued to work on brand awareness and fundraising and Stephen was instrumental in developing the charity to heights that none of us could have imagined just five years before.

YLF not only became well known throughout the county but was also the beneficiary of the Queen's Award for Volunteering. The board had suggested that we hold the ceremony at Leeds Castle but in recognition of the support we had always received from Turrloo Parrett of Eastwell Manor, I persuaded them to hold the event there and undertook to arrange everything myself. When I rang Turrloo to ask for a commercial quote he offered the room, canopies and complimentary wine for a nominal price – such a generous man. The award was presented by the Lord Lieutenant, Viscount Philip De L'Isle, in front of 100 guests.

The tenth anniversary was certainly one worth celebrating and we needed a good speaker. I spoke to Helen Grant MP, who kindly pulled a few strings and arranged for the

Children and Families Minister, Robert Goodwill to join us at Allington Castle, the home of my friend Sir Robert Worcester, who not only donated the venue but also the dinner – such generosity once again.

I stepped down as chairman after ten years. My expertise is in getting organisations off the ground and once running smoothly, it takes a different mindset to keep the authorities happy with governance and due process. Geoff took over and doubled the size of the board, while I resigned as a trustee to take on the role of president and I still assist with fundraising.

Until I became involved, I didn't realise the chasm in thinking between business and charity. On the whole it was an amazing ten years – we got things done – and with the combination of knowing the right people and caring for the underprivileged, I truly think we made a significant difference to a great number of lives.

I am pleased to say that the charity continues to go from strength to strength under Stephen's excellent stewardship and that 250 volunteers give 34,000 hours every year to look after 3,500 vulnerable children and families in Kent.

Being the figurehead of the charity was no doubt instrumental in my being awarded an MBE for services to vulnerable children in Kent but, as always, I was just part of an amazing team which makes such a difference.

CHAPTER 16

CHARITY AUCTION MEMORIES

Over the years I have been asked to conduct charity auctions for many different causes. Although I try to concentrate my energies on those benefiting vulnerable young children, I find it difficult to look at a blank page in my diary and decide not to help a worthy cause. All charities struggle to raise funds and it is a privilege to be asked to help.

I reckon that I have auctioned well over £5 million-worth of lots for various organisations over the years. As the demand has increased, I now tend to concentrate my appearances in Kent and East Sussex while my colleagues do the ones further afield and in their own operating areas.

Most are relatively straightforward and vary from well-organised, high-value items to some that are no more than a glorified jumble sale. But to the organisers they are all important and the subject of much hard work behind the scenes.

I now have a mini contract that I send to the organiser before agreeing to attend an event. That might sound a bit arrogant, but it's the result of some horrendous experiences, such as being put on after the raffle, when everyone just wants to go home, or during the meal when the supporters are concentrating on their food and chatting to fellow guests.

I also refuse to conduct an auction where the lots have not been fully gifted. There is a growing culture of employing a company to provide the prizes, usually on the condition that they also hold a silent auction in the same venue. The deal is that the promotional company deducts the cost of the item to be auctioned before giving the balance of the hammer price to the charity. For example, a signed photograph/cricket bat/boxing glove/racing helmet might sell for £700, £500 of which goes to the company and just £200 to the charity.

The buyer, of course, is unaware of the agreement and in their mind has given a donation to the charity of £700 and 'done their bit.' Furthermore, why should I, as a professional auctioneer, use my talents to sell commercial goods *pro bono* and be complicit in depriving worthy causes of money that they so desperately need? Most of the lots can be bought far cheaper on the internet anyway.

On one occasion I was asked to take the rostrum at a charity dinner at the House of Commons. I arrived at 7pm to be told that I was a bit early but could wait in an ante-room while they had dinner. They were somewhat taken aback when I told them that I had just given up my evening, travelled up from Kent at my own expense and if a meal was too much trouble, then I might as well head back. Luckily, one of the guests dropped out at the last minute so I could sit at his table. There are times when I elect to attend after the dinner just to conduct the auction, but these are generally local venues on days where I am expected elsewhere beforehand – and it's also my choice.

I often get booked early in the year to conduct charity auctions in December, a particularly busy time in the calendar with the last professional sale of the year, promotional parties and drinks invitations, after-lunch and dinner speeches as well as the social engagements which Sue and I always enjoyed attending together.

One year I double-booked a Saturday evening by entering in the diary 'old folks charity auction.' A few days before the allotted evening I received a call from one of the organisers to run through the lots to be offered. 'I did that yesterday,' I replied and went ashen when I realised my mistake. I had agreed to conduct the auction for Bobby, a long-standing friend of mine for his old people's charity on the same night as I had booked for Andrew, another friend from school days, for the old people's charity he was supporting. One was in Maidstone, the other in Sevenoaks – some twenty miles away – and with the timings there was no way I could do both. I asked around our open-plan office if anyone would step in to take one of them. No one could do it – they were either babysitting, watching a football match or had friends coming round.

In the end James said OK, he would do it if no one else would – he was concentrating at the time on promoting the Brighton branch and did more than his fair share there, but with the absence of any other volunteers I gratefully accepted his offer. He elected to take the Maidstone event as he knew Bobby and his family well.

When the catalogue came through, one of the lots was a visit to the Aston Martin Factory to try out the different models on their test track for a day. James mentioned that he would bid for that lot up to £500. Although it's difficult to predict with charity auctions, I knew that might not be enough, so I rang Bobby and asked him to bid on the lot for me without James knowing and sent him a blank cheque to cover the cost. I told him not to miss it for the sake of a few quid, but not to go mad!

The next morning, I rang James to see how he got on and he said it was a good evening, the auction raised £18,000 and added, 'You wouldn't believe what Bobby paid for the Aston Martin Day – what a plonker!'

I just said that Bobby was an Aston Martin fan and left it at that. When I received the voucher, I put it on the Christmas tree for James with a note 'from one plonker to another.' He didn't need to open it to know what was inside. After Christmas, one of the auctioneers in the office said that he would have loved to have gone and rather cheekily I replied, 'You've got to be in it to win it – maybe you would be better going to a football match.' A cheap jibe, but it made me feel better.

James' kind offer left me free to take the Sevenoaks auction for Andrew. To my surprise, nowhere did it acknowledge, either in the menu or on the list of lots, that I was the honorary auctioneer. In the final speech, the chairman thanked the committee, the venue, the caterers, the volunteers, the supporters, the flower lady, even the car park attendants – but no mention of the auctioneer who had helped raise £13,000.

Although we don't attend the auctions to seek public gratitude, we are running a business and part of the role in attending charity events is a way of promoting the business or, as it is commonly called, raising brand awareness. On my way to the car park, one of the guests came over to say I should do auctions for a living and when told that I did, asked if I was from one of our competitors. Point made.

The following year Andrew asked if I would do the same auction again and when I explained the reasons why I wouldn't be repeating the experience, he rather naively exclaimed, 'But surely, everyone knows you?' A seasoned businessman whom I'd known since schooldays and who had run an extremely successful company had missed the point entirely as 'I had apparently appeared to enjoy being there.' How else would one behave? Having said that, he is one of the loveliest, caring people I know. He just didn't quite get it on this occasion.

The majority of events, whether held at a lunch or dinner, are most enjoyable but they do take a chunk out of the diary when I could be generating fee income for the company. I decided some time ago that I wouldn't do any more London auctions as it usually involves leaving the office halfway through the afternoon in black tie and returning in the early hours of the next day, knackered. We do very little business in central London, there are plenty of good and bad, large and small, property and fine art auctioneers up there so no shortage of local people to step in if asked.

Another one of my good friends once rang me in Spain to ask if I would do an auction for him in London and when I declined, insisted that he wanted me to take the rostrum. I first met Harry at a Tunbridge Wells Taverners do and a more generous, gentle and philanthropic person it would be hard to find. He would not take no for an answer. He was the Crown Jeweller and the Queen's personal jeweller. Harry told me that he had just taken over the role of Chairman of the Prince's International Trust, the event was to be held at the Long Room at Lord's in the presence of the Duke of Edinburgh and, no doubt based on the knowledge that flattery will get you everywhere, finished by saying that he wanted the auction to be in a safe pair of hands.

'Sorry, I thought you said London,' I replied. 'Of course I will be delighted to go the renowned Long Room to help and anyway, that's not really London is it?'

Pre-dinner drinks for the committee, speakers and VIPs were held in an ante-room where the Duke would meet a ready-formed group of six to eight people at a time.

How royalty must get fed up with chatting to small groups with fixed smiles laughing nervously at nothing. HRH had arrived in his personal Balmoral green London cab which he used to get around London on non-ceremonial events. When I mentioned it, he said that it was nice to travel incognito, to which I replied, 'If it wasn't for the two motorcycle outriders and the Range Rover with machine guns behind the darkened windows, no one would know.'

More importantly, I asked how many cricket bats he had signed, to which the reply was, 'I don't think I have signed a cricket bat in my life.'

Not the answer I wanted.

'Well, that's a bugger, I'm selling one tonight with your signature on it. Is it a forgery, sir?'

He winked at me and said he might have signed one a bit earlier.

His equerry came up after the Duke had moved on to say that most people chose their language a bit more carefully when addressing His Royal Highness. I told him that as a professional auctioneer, I needed to know; a rare signature will fetch more money and to offer a forgery would be illegal. And anyway, I was sure that having been in the Navy, he would have heard far worse.

The auction went exceptionally well and the cricket bat signed by the England and Australian teams and the Duke of Edinburgh made £28,000 – a record at the time. It was bought by a wealthy American who had flown over especially for the dinner and he was delighted to have a photo of HRH handing the bat to him, which probably takes pride of place in his office in the States. I have to say that this was one of the very rare times I was nervous; the Duke just created an aura in a room that is difficult to explain. I couldn't have blotted my copy book too badly, however, as I was invited back to the next dinner, which this time was hosted by Prince Edward.

Selling in front of royalty is unusual but not unheard of although, generally, the fundraising bit is done after they have departed. In 1989 I was asked to take the auction in Ashford for Riding for the Disabled. It was held at the recently opened Ashford International Hotel and HRH Princess Royal was attending as President of the charity. She arrived by helicopter, looking radiant and immaculate – almost as if she had been in the bath all afternoon – but in fact, it was her fifth appearance that day.

As with all royal visits, the timetable is to the minute: 19.22 helicopter lands, 19.24 HRH alights, 19.26 HRH enters the room, etc. On our running sheet HRH was to leave at 22.08 for the helicopter to take off at 22.12. We had a nice chat in the green room, nothing too controversial but she genuinely seemed interested in what the guests were saying – or maybe that was just wishful thinking.

One of the lots was a painting by Prince Charles, which had been donated. I advised the organisers to get it underwritten at £3,000 or so – nothing more embarrassing than little sister telling her brother that his picture made just a few hundred quid! There was no need for such concern as it sold for £4,500; it must have been the future King's signature. The real problem arose when the organisers asked me to take the auction at 21.50 as they were running well ahead of time, but just fifteen minutes before the planned royal departure.

I went over and asked HRH if she intended leaving on schedule, to which she replied, 'I haven't made up my mind yet.' Apparently, one is not supposed to ask royalty a direct question, but how the hell you find the answer without asking still escapes me. Having said that, I learned at the age of eight that if you don't want the answer to be 'no,' don't ask the question; the penalty for ignorance is usually less severe than for disobedience.

However, this needed to be sorted so I explained, 'We are both here, are we not, free of charge, to raise as much as we can for your charity? If you leave during the auction the disturbance will inevitably have a negative effect on the amount raised.'

I had met my match for sure as she came back with, 'If I am amused, I will stay, if not I won't.'

I suppose I'd asked for it, but I left saying, 'No pressure then, Ma'am.'

Shepherd Neame, the oldest local brewery in the country, had donated a bottle of vintage port which sold for an amazing price. I did remark when describing it that, as Kent's leading brewery, they could have at least donated a new bottle. When the buyer came to collect it, HRH said that he must love his port to which he replied, rather pathetically I thought, 'No Ma'am – I just wanted to shake your hand' at which she raised her eyes to the sky and remarked that there were far cheaper ways than that! My God, she was on good form that evening, since when I have had nothing but utter respect and admiration for her.

Dealing with hecklers in the audience is an occupational hazard and, in my view, can add sparkle to the occasion, as long as they are not too drunk or stupid. A professional auctioneer should be able to respond to most comments and retain the upper hand, if only because the auctioneer is sober, standing and has a microphone to override comments from the floor. The difficulty can arise when the organiser feels duty-bound to interfere during the sale.

I was taking the rostrum for the Wooden Spoon annual dinner (the rugby equivalent to the Taverners and cricket) when their President, a former England rugby union and Harlequins and Blackheath player, jumped on to the rostrum to help me identify the bids and comment on the lots. He was full of his own self-importance, fuelled either by alcohol or a massive misplaced ego, and behaved like a complete pain in the arse. After a couple of requests for him to leave the podium, I changed tack.

'I'll tell you what,' I said, 'why don't you sell the next lot and I'll watch closely to learn how to do it?'

The audience loved the sarcasm, but he took it seriously and said it would be his pleasure. As with most amateurs, he spent far too long describing what he was about to offer and when the first bid came in from a regular and generous buyer, he said, 'No, I'm not taking your bid, you buy everything, it's not about you, it's about the children, so give someone else a chance.' Unbelievable!

Pat took it in his stride – he was there to support the charity, as he did with so many others that he attended. I was particularly offended as he is a good and loyal friend whom I first met at a Round Table boxing match at the Great Danes Hotel some years ago when I was virtually booed off stage as the drunken crowd was baying for the strippers to come on.

A jolly Irishman, successful property developer and quarry owner, Pat met me in the bar and apologised for the behaviour of the crowd – not that it was his fault, he was also a guest. He was mortified at my treatment and we got to know each other over a few double scotches. I was advised later that I would have more chance of beating John McEnroe at tennis than drinking Pat under the table. And how right that proved. The last thing I remember was falling backwards over a low coffee table and waking up at midday in one of the hotel rooms with the worst headache and hangover I have ever had, either before or since. Since that evening Pat and I have been really good friends and meet up very regularly for lunch or a day at the races. He also has a villa in Marbella not far from ours. You can imagine just how angry I was at the way my friend had been treated by the President.

When I had finished the auction, I said to Micky, 'I reckon I could get £1,500 for your waistcoat,' which was one he'd had specially made from his England Rugby shirt. He protested that it was very special to him, but I insisted that it wasn't about him, it was about the children.

'Maybe next year,' came the response, to which I replied, 'No, Micky, the children need the money now.'

He whipped off the waistcoat and threw it to me, saying, 'If it doesn't make £1,500, I keep it.' Clearly it meant a lot to him. When I offered the waistcoat, I said to the audience, 'You've heard the conversation – do I see £1,500 for it?'

Like a shot Pat shouted, 'I'll give £1,500 as long as I don't have to wear it!'

Job done. Pat did take it with him and later put it into another charity auction. Everyone, apart from Micky , of course, was very happy with the result.

I am often asked what is the most bizarre thing I have ever sold and the answer has to be a vasectomy donated by a surgeon at a hospital charity auction in Canterbury. The icing on the cake was when I pointed out to a chap laughing his head off that I didn't know why he was laughing – the purchaser was his wife. At the same auction I sold a signed cricket bat to a chap who has seven daughters in the days before women took to the wicket. His wife was furious and hopefully didn't get hold of the bat on their return home.

Charity auctions can bring fun and laughter but also utter frustration. I don't think I am being paranoid about being messed about, but sometimes it really takes the patience of all charity auctioneers to the limit. I was asked to conduct an auction at Rochester Cathedral at a major fundraising dinner in the nave for 200 people in the presence of HRH Sophie Wessex, Patron of the Cathedral. The event was scheduled for the first week in October – right in the middle of our annual holiday with friends in Spain. With Sue's blessing I rearranged the flights and our guests rescheduled their visits. The cathedral is a good cause and very special to me.

Some weeks before the event the Dean rang full of remorse and apologies to say that the then Lord Lieutenant of Kent, Philip De L'Isle, had decreed that it would be inappropriate to conduct an auction in front of royalty. I asked The Dean if the actual word used had been vulgar! At a drinks do in the Deanery gardens a few days later I pointed out that I had sold at events attended by Princess Anne, Edward and the Duke of Edinburgh twice, the second at his request. Clearly surprised, and relieved, the Dean said he would mention it at the meeting the following evening, chaired by the Lord Lieutenant. He rang to say the answer was still no – he could not believe the stubbornness. I said, 'Don't worry, just ask him to donate the £15,000 we would have probably raised', a suggestion that was received with some mirth. There are so many cases where those with inherited wealth have no idea just how much time and effort is expended by 'ordinary' people to keep charities afloat.

Sadly, due to the pandemic, charity auctions, along with commercial sales, have been prevented from taking place. It will be a welcome return to normal when the fundraising process can continue once again to fill the coffers of such deserving causes.

CHAPTER 17

THE HOT-AIR BALLOON

Being asked to conduct charity auctions, *pro bono* of course, is an occupational hazard. There have been many evenings when I have left Sue sitting by a lovely fire burning in the inglenook to travel all over Kent to host a charity auction. I have met some fascinating people and enjoyed some spectacular events, but I've also experienced some that were the exact opposite. One never knows, however, what will come from such occasions.

One that proved particularly memorable was when I was asked by a chartered surveyor friend of mine to attend the PTA auction evening at his daughter's school in Tonbridge. It was one of those occasions when nobody really wanted to be there, including me; the audience was neither keen to give nor to buy any of the 100 or so pathetic lots on offer.

It was held in a large hall without a PA system and with people eating and drinking at their tables and chatting away while I was trying to capture their attention – an absolute nightmare. One of the lots was an hour in a private swimming pool with a glass of wine, not even the bloody bottle.

I eventually brought the hammer down hard on the rostrum and said, 'Can I remind you that I am here, free of charge, so that your privileged children can go on a holiday, which you are calling a sports trip, so that some other bugger will pay for it. So, may I have your attention please?'

Well, as you can imagine, the room went completely quiet after that and the next lot, half a dozen free-range eggs, sold for a magnificent £22. I asked the buyer if she was sure and 'Yes – whatever you say,' came the nervous reply. The Headmistress asked if I could come back on Monday morning as she'd never seen the room so attentive.

After the auction finished, a chap came up to me and asked why I did it for nothing, which is a question I've asked myself on many an occasion. Anyway, he said he was the donor of the hot-air balloon flight and that he'd like to take me up as a thank you. I gave him my card and expected to hear no more. Keith rang three times to arrange a flight, which eventually took off one evening from Bodiam Castle. It was my first hot-air balloon flight and I enjoyed it very much.

While we were talking in the pub afterwards, Keith mentioned that he was going to Thailand the following spring with a number of other balloonists.

'What if the wind changes?' I asked. He didn't quite get my sense of humour and painstakingly explained that the balloon and basket would be shipped over.

Some two months later I got a call from Keith to say that one of the crew could no longer join the group to Thailand and would I like to go in his place? Up until then my holidays were limited to Dymchurch and Malaga. Sue didn't like flying, but for the sake of the family undertook short journeys of no more than two hours – hence Malaga, which is where we have a villa.

As always, I asked Sue what she thought.

'Well,' she said, 'long-haul and balloons are not my thing, but why don't you go?'

I pointed out that there were another twenty-nine balloon anoraks on the trip, none of whom I'd met before and what if they didn't like me?

'It will be a long ten days for them then,' she replied. Sue always had a lovely way of keeping my feet on the ground.

Anyway, I decided to go and duly arrived at the airport. Although I prefer to fly Club Class, I bought a standard ticket in order not to alienate myself from the others before we had even left the UK. Keith told me that all tickets had been booked separately and if I wanted to upgrade, nobody would have a problem, so that's what I did. The air stewardess went through the usual safety routine, ending up by saying, "If the pilot says "brace, brace", you must put your head between your legs,' to which the guy behind me remarked, 'If I could do that I wouldn't be going to Thailand.' It was also refreshing to be told that if this 400-seater, double-deck airliner put down in the ocean and the ships around us hadn't noticed, that we had a light and whistle to attract their attention.

I felt like a child on his first day at school; was I wearing the right clothes, standing in the right queue, pitching the jokes at the right level? I soon realised once the balloon was launched for the first time just why I had been invited – when inflating the envelope, someone of strength and size has to hold on to the crown rope to hold the top of the balloon down. With my weight behind the rope, it was going nowhere.

The trip was amazing and I immediately loved Thailand and its gentle, attentive people. The police were not quite so friendly. On the very first flight the wind direction changed and we were blown across the main flight path into Chiang Mai airport. Massive airliners were having to circle until we were out of the way. As we were coming into land, there were four police trucks at each corner of the field. I mentioned to Keith that they didn't look too happy.

'Oh, you worry too much Clive – they've probably just never seen a balloon before.'

The police were indeed taking photos of the balloon, but apparently were not amused when I took a photo of them – another lesson learned. We were told to follow them to the police station with the balloon, which was now deflated and back in the trailer. An intimidating and dirty place, it was four hours before we were released, having paid a hefty fine and been told never to fly in the region again. It had been a long way to go for just one flight.

It was decided that we would travel north by road in the four-seater cab trucks to Chiang Rai, some five hours away. Alternatively, for just £50 we could catch a private plane flown by a German to Chiang Rai Airport. The price should have been a bit of a giveaway. When we arrived, the pilot took one look at me and decided to take the bigger plane parked at the back of a makeshift hangar.

He blew up the left tyre and jump-started the engine as the battery was flat. While we were taxiing down the grass runway, the bonnet flew open where he'd not fastened it properly when accessing the battery. He got out, closed the bonnet and returned to the beginning of the runway to prepare for another take-off. We seemed to be on the ground for a long time and when I queried this, he told me the flaps didn't work so it took a bit longer to get airborne.

Once in the air he tapped the instrument panel and told us that he'd forgotten that the dial didn't work either.

'Is it important?' I asked in as as casual a voice as I could muster.

'Oh no,' he replied breezily. 'It's only the altimeter – and we can see the ground down there.'

Of course, when we arrived at Chiang Rai, we had to take a low-entry approach to the runway as the flaps weren't working. The whole flight had certainly saved the need for laxatives.

The rest of the trip was relatively uneventful but did include spectacular flying over paddy fields, forests and the famous River Kwai. We had to take off either at dawn or dusk when the wind levels were best and spent our days relaxing by the pool or going on tours.

However, what I will never forget is the poverty and desperation of the residents of Burma. We crossed the bridge on one outing and the memory of those starving, feral children will stay with me forever. We were told not to give them money as it would only be spent by their minders on drugs. Despite being told that they were made to look hungry to beg for help, it was perfectly obvious that you can't look emaciated during the day and well fed in the evening. Such a cruel world.

The next year Keith phoned to say that the balloon fest would be in Austria and I would be joining them, wouldn't I? As we planned to drive to Austria, Sue joined me on the trip. I am not sure what heaven might be like, but ballooning in the mountains in the morning and skiing in the afternoon has to be pretty close to utopia. During a drink-fuelled dinner one evening, Keith mentioned that the team was going to South Africa the following year, flying over Rorke's Drift and travelling from Cape Town to Johannesburg. Sadly, however, his balloon envelope was now ten years old and wouldn't be suitable for the extreme changes in temperature.

'What if I bought a new balloon envelope in the Clive Emson colours and you fly it with your basket?' I suggested in an alcoholic haze. It was something that appealed to us both; when in the UK, Keith flew in our operational area in Sussex and it would be an excellent and memorable advert for the company. Keith was relaxed about the dominating logo – he wouldn't be able to see it from below – and I phoned James the next morning to ask him to add £15,000 to our non-existent promotional budget. When I told him what we'd agreed, I could sense the feeling of despair from the other end of the line.

'£15,000 won't do it – I'll put aside £20,000.'

How right he was.

The envelope was designed and made in Bristol and has since raised several tens of thousands of pounds for charity; we often throw in a free flight at charity auctions and speculate just what a hot-air balloon and an auctioneer could possibly have in common…

The next year our visit to South Africa proved both fascinating and relatively uneventful, apart from nearly taking the roof off a Zulu temple and landing in a game reserve. I was on retrieval that particular morning, which is when you follow the balloon in the truck with a trailer to collect it on landing. Getting the ranger to allow me into the reserve was a challenge and when I got to the balloon it was surrounded not by tigers, but by teenage Zulu boys, who were really rather intimidating.

There is quite a lot of expensive equipment in a balloon basket, so Keith just released some of the butane gas. It made a high-pitched hissing noise and all of a sudden, the boys disappeared into the long grass. However, we knew they were still there watching us – just like the scene in that famous Rorke's Drift film *Zulu*.

During the journey from Cape Town to Joburg we stayed at a hotel in Bethlehem and when I asked the receptionist whether I should turn left or right out of the door for my evening stroll, I was politely informed that if we wanted to continue the journey in the morning, we would be better off staying in the building.

The excursion to Lesotho was one of the most frightening I've experienced, eclipsing even the flight from Chiang Mai to Chiang Rai. Lesotho is set on a high plateau at the top of the mountain and the only way up there is via a crumbling, twisting track which they laughingly call a road. The bald tyres on the really old, open trucks were perilously close to the edge of a vertical drop of several hundred feet as the caravans going up and down passed each other. I took solace in the fact that our middle-aged driver hadn't fallen off yet, although there was plenty of evidence of others who had.

Some time later, I was at the wedding in Hythe of Eric's son Ben to Liz when one of my friends came up to the table and said there was a guest over from South Africa asking what a Clive Emson was? She had a photo of the balloon on her phone which she'd taken when we landed in the paddock adjoining her house and couldn't believe that, having travelled all that way from Cape Town to Kent, the owner was sitting just a few feet away.

The next year we were back in Austria, but the snow was so heavy that there was only one flight and the lifts were closed. Instead, Sue and I hightailed it off to Serre Chevalier where the slopes are better groomed and we had a lot of friends.

The last trip abroad with the balloon was to the Loire Valley, where six teams from a party of twenty-four enthusiasts descended on the area to fly over the beautiful countryside in ideal conditions. My leg was giving me some pain on the way down, which I initially thought was a rare attack of gout. I was in a delirious fever, going from boiling hot to shivering cold that night and the next day my leg blew up to twice its size.

Keith, a dentist by profession and one of the wives who is a nurse, insisted that I visit the local doctor. Before I knew it, I was admitted to hospital with cellulitis, an extremely painful and quite dangerous infection. On being admitted the male nurse thought I was of a similar persuasion, probably a misunderstanding in translation as I said when I entered, 'Je suis fatigue,' which he took to mean that I was an overweight homosexual. He said I might feel a small prick, to which I responded that I was really not interested, so he stuck a needle in me. As I was coming round, I felt his hand under the sheet and him saying, 'C'est magnifique' – how disappointed he seemed when I said he was pulling my leg.

Every day I was told I might be released tomorrow. I was admitted on Monday and by Friday there was little improvement. A really sweet night nurse from California told me that I would probably be in for another two weeks. The hospital was some twenty miles from the hotel and the next day the party would be returning to the UK, leaving Sue stranded on her own. I had taken my Rolls-Royce Corniche convertible on the tour, which was too big for her to drive.

One of the balloonists had a private light aircraft close by and offered to fly Sue and me home, where I could at least be treated by my own doctor and be close to the family. Charlie, my loyal driver, agreed to bring the Range Rover to Lydd airport and return to France in the plane to bring back the Rolls. For someone who hated flying, Sue did brilliantly and actually enjoyed the journey at the low level we flew. I saw my doctor at 8.30am on the Monday and he told me I should not have discharged myself. I was quite ill and was admitted as an emergency to the local hospital within the hour.

A lovely, bow-tie wearing doctor in the clinical decision unit at the William Harvey Hospital correctly speculated that I was in an environment with which I was not totally familiar. I was transferred to the Chaucer private hospital that day, again by ambulance, although I did say that Sue would be happy to give me a lift. There I remained for the next three weeks, having been told that I could have lost my leg and that if the infection had spread, the sepsis would have been life-threatening.

I still fly on occasions in the UK, but prefer to let those less fortunate than myself share a wonderful experience when possible.

What a lot of fun and amazing experiences came from a little charity auction which I hadn't really wanted to attend. It just goes to show, once again, that life is what you make it.

CHAPTER 18

NOT EVERYTHING GOES TO PLAN

One of my wealthier buyers attended an auction held at The Great Danes Hotel near Maidstone back in 2004. He had travelled from Stamford Hill with his son Joel, who was over from New York. David was a seasoned and respected property professional with the record for buying the most expensive lot we had ever sold at that time.

After the auction, David told me they didn't hold ballroom-style sales like this in New York and he thought it was a formula that might catch on. After further discussions, it was agreed we would look into forming a partnership under the Clive Emson banner to hold sales in the States.

James and I flew over to assess the situation. Joel impressed on us that he knew all the right people, including Donald Trump, and was confident that he could get the lots if we would handle the admin side and conduct the sale on the day. Naturally, I was conscious that we might be punching above our weight, but because it was an avenue that we might regret not exploring if another firm made a real success of it, decided we should proceed with caution.

We were careful to ring-fence the American partnership to keep the UK business safe and so franchised the Clive Emson name to the new venture. Joel secured an office suite in the Empire State building and another subsidiary office in Brooklyn.

On our second visit we met the lawyers. In the States these guys are all-powerful and certainly know how to complicate even the simplest of procedures. We were told that as auctioneers, we could not hold the deposit – that was the attorney's job. Furthermore, only the client could sign the contract. Following discussion, it emerged that the reasoning for the deposit was not enshrined in law but was there because more than 40 per cent of commission claims in the USA were challenged. All the more reason for us to hold the deposit; I would certainly prefer to be sued than sue.

I questioned why the client had to sign the contract and what would happen if they couldn't attend or refused to do so after the fall of the hammer. Our letter of engagement in the UK gives us irrevocable authority to sign on the client's behalf at or above the agreed reserve. Apparently, the client needing to sign the contract was the lawyer's solution to protect us from litigation in case we made a mistake.

After much time and debate, we managed to establish that we could sign on the client's behalf if they could not attend. I argued that if we could sign then, I saw no reason why we couldn't do so in all cases. There was no argument to that and so we agreed that we would sign the contract and hold the deposit. All sounds very straightforward, but it took four hours to agree those two issues.

The other issue was the agency agreement which, in the UK, we keep to ten clauses in bold type on two sides of A4. The lawyers managed to expand it to fourteen pages of close type, which had the obvious effect; a client would want his attorney to agree it before entering a lot and of course, the seller's lawyer would try to negotiate changes, wasting valuable marketing time. In the end I persuaded Joel that we would go with the UK version and take the risk that we might be challenged after the sale, something that would be highly unlikely if we actually performed in accordance with the agreement.

The meeting room was on the 65th floor of the Empire State Building, but as it was an internal room it might just have well been in the basement. I soon realised that Joel was all about image; the fact that we were collected from JFK in a stretch limo should have alerted me. We would have been quite happy in a yellow cab, which I insisted we use for future journeys.

Son-in-law Steve, our computer guru, went to the States to set up the auction programme which would be connected to our servers and monitored in the UK. I spent many weeks in New York accompanied by a small team that included James, our UK Kent office manager Gill, Hilary our company secretary and my friend Roger, who had experience in setting up new businesses abroad.

Joel was a novice at auctions and many of the trips were to train him and his team on the method and protocol of property auctions. I mentioned that we would be better having fewer realistically priced lots than a full book of unsaleable properties. Auctioneers are known for their success rate as much as anything and so 80 per cent of thirty lots would be better than 25 per cent of 100 lots. Unsold lots also affect the bottom line; we survive on commission and unsold lots cost us money.

The first catalogue was typeset in the UK and printed in the States. Everything became a chore. The templates for America had to be reset as the paper size is different, the spelling is different, the descriptions are different, the measurements are different – definitely a case of two cultures separated by a common language.

The catalogue for the inaugural sale on 22 March 2005 was duly published with thirty lots that would apparently definitely sell. I rang Joel four days after the mailout expressing concern that the statistics I was getting were not compatible with those experienced in the UK. I was told that the Americans are different, but I reminded him that the motivation on both sides of the pond usually involves an element of greed.

The next day I rang again to reiterate my concern and was assured there was no problem. I wasn't happy so caught the midnight flight from Heathrow, which arrived at 9am New York time the next day. As I entered the Brooklyn office, I noticed around 3,000 of the 4,500 catalogues which we had printed stacked against a wall in reception. In the States, magazines are not sent in envelopes or plastic bags, as the label is stuck to the cover for mailing. With our catalogue the return address was closer to the stamp than the label and so we sent out 4,000 catalogues only to receive 3,000 back at the office the following day.

I asked Joel rather forcefully that if he didn't see that as a problem, then I would hate to know what he did consider a problem. It was now too late to reschedule the sale – the team of fifteen from the UK, the staging and the hotel had all been booked. Postponement was not an option.

We agreed that Joel and his team would get on the phone to his contacts and resend some of the catalogues to those potential bidders in a sealed envelope. Not a good start, but, once again, I was assured that all was in hand and no need to worry.

With Joel's help and contacts, I was able to obtain a daytime auctioneer's licence to sell in New York and we selected the Park Lane Hotel on Fifth Avenue as our venue. We wanted the first auction to be impressive, as a UK company coming to town to teach the Americans how to sell by auction was likely to be a high-profile event.

The advertising was extensive. Keith Rogans rang me to say that he had popped over for a few days shopping with his wife and saw our enormous revolving advert on the illuminated billboard at Times Square, the New York equivalent of Piccadilly Circus. Good for the ego and brand awareness, but I wasn't convinced how many lots it would actually sell.

The day of the auction finally arrived and the team from Kent was there to set up the saleroom. Joel had organised some scantily dressed usherettes to direct the bidders to the auction, which was held on the first floor. There was a buzz of expectation in the room and we appeared to sell 80 per cent of the catalogue. Four days after the sale, I rang Brooklyn to ask where the deposits were as they hadn't yet appeared on the computer. Imagine, if you can, my shock at hearing from Joel that he had planted bidders in the room to make the sale look good but that there were no funds to pay the deposits, let alone complete on the transactions. It was a disaster – just four of the thirty lots had sold to genuine buyers.

Not only were we taking valuable staff away from our established and successful operation in the UK but we were risking serious damage to our reputation of twenty years standing. The venture had cost us serious money and we had to decide whether to invest more funds and install a completely new team or withdraw with our tail between our legs. As with all things, if you cannot trust your partner there is no hope of a future. We decided to withdraw from New York and I rang David to inform him of our decision as matter of courtesy.

Joel was summoned from America and David asked for a meeting one Sunday morning to retrieve the situation. I did suggest that he spoke to Joel to establish the facts behind our decision and he assured me that he was *au fait* with what had happened. At the meeting he was astonished to hear my version of events, which Joel could not deny, and we agreed to sell our share to him for one dollar. He could keep the computers and assets in Brooklyn and our name would not be used again, with immediate effect.

Although commercially a disaster, it was an experience I have never regretted. It is always so much easier not to take a chance, but at the time the opportunity did seem to be a logical progression. However, had the business taken off it would have been only three years before the US property crash caused by toxic loans and we might well have lost everything then.

The strain on our core business and pressure for the UK team was lifted, my DVT (brought on by all those trips to New York) prevented me from flying long haul and so we decided that from now on the UK was where our future should be for expansion. I still see David from time to time but the New York experience is a subject that we tend to avoid; it's no good looking back when there is such a good future ahead.

Like so many other people I know, it's often a big mistake venturing into new areas outside one's comfort zone or, more importantly, area of expertise.

In 1973 I opened my new estate agency branch in Hythe (now operating under the Ward & Partners banner). In those days all agents spent a considerable amount on advertising in the local press. It was one of those things everybody did, because they'd always done so. Seldom was a sale made from this medium; if they were serious, a buyer would have visited the various offices in the vicinity of their search rather than wait to see what was available in a restricted list of properties for sale in the local paper. And, of course, there was no internet in those days. The main point of the advertising was to appease the sellers, who want to see visible proof that you are trying to find a buyer.

By 1979 I took the view that if a potential seller wanted to choose his agent because of local advertising, then they would go for the biggest display, which single-office agents were certainly not offering. My answer was to persuade sellers that rather than waste money on a newspaper advert, they would be better off placing in our window a half-plate (6x4in), full-colour picture of their house together with some interior shots. After all, it's where serious potential buyers tend to start their search. At that time, nearly every agent relied on rather small and tatty Polaroid photos, which produced an immediate picture, albeit in grainy black and white.

One of the tenants at The Old Post Office, where I had established my auction room, was a photographer who developed his own film, so I agreed a special deal with him that mine were the only agent's photos he would process and that they would be returned within twelve hours. This gave me a definite commercial advantage over my competitors, who would wait three days for Boots to return their pictures or, more likely, somebody else's holiday snaps. This was in the days of rolls of film and there was often a further delay while using up the film before it could be sent off for processing – and then the result would be small photos rather than impressive larger images.

The initiative brought in extra business as anyone looking in the different agents' windows to decide which one to appoint tended to come to me as my displays were head and shoulders above the others. This system worked for four years until I sold my business to Ward & Partners, at which point my photographer tenant told me that he wanted to buy a new machine which would produce multiple colour mini pictures. Agents could then attach these to all their sales particulars.

Rather than lend him the money, I agreed to buy his business, Harbour Photographics, and employ George as manager and his small team. This was a tax-efficient way of acquiring the new machine but, in hindsight, it would have been better just to have given him the money.

As with any business, volume is essential to benefit from the economies of scale. We bought a BMW motorcycle and employed a dispatch rider to collect films from across Kent during the day and George would develop them overnight and the pictures would be returned to the agent before noon the next day. It was a unique service and we built up a substantial client list. The more agents we had on board, the more efficient and cost-effective was the dispatch rider. Jo Williams, a close friend and legendary within the world of sales, visited the agents to sell the concept and increase the volumes.

All good news apart from one issue – despite the turnover, we were making a loss. The cost of materials was only just short of the cost of the sales. When asked, George stressed that there was inevitable wastage at the beginning and end of a film called the 'run-off.' Not being in the industry, I couldn't argue with him, but after making enquiries with other processors, I knew there must be a bigger problem somewhere, but I just couldn't fathom out where the shrinkage had evolved. Sue and I dealt with all the banking and invoices, which meant it was not an accounting fraud.

One night I woke at 2am and decided to go to the studio to see for myself where savings could be made. On arrival the door was locked and I could get no reply to my knocking, despite hearing the machines whirring away inside. I took the sledgehammer from the back of my car, which I kept there to re-erect for sale boards that needed attention on my travels, and aimed at the door lock.

As the door flew open the team looked not only shocked, but highly embarrassed. I could immediately see the problem. As well as lots of pictures of houses, there was an equal number of pornographic pictures of girls in all sorts of poses. Presumably, it was a lucrative trade – there was no internet in those days and only the odd top-shelf magazine for those wishing to indulge in such viewing.

Where George got the film and who he was selling to was not my immediate concern, the real issue was that it was my business, I was a well-known local businessman and would anyone really believe that this was going on without my knowledge and that I wasn't benefiting from the exploitation of young women? The headlines in the local paper would have been damaging beyond repair.

I sacked the whole team on the spot and turned off the machines. I employed the dispatch rider for one more trip to tell the agents who had supported us that the service was no longer operating. One saving grace was that the business was fronted by George and no one else was aware of my involvement.

I couldn't leave the pictures on the floor for anyone to see, so I put them in a couple of black plastic bags and kept them in the loft at home as evidence in the event of being sued for unfair dismissal. Because the machines were switched off with the chemicals still inside, they were damaged beyond repair. The whole affair was a commercial disaster, but a valuable lesson in sticking to what you know and even more importantly, that the most charismatic partner can be a crook and exploit his benefactor.

When I went to the attic to retrieve the films for burning some five years later, they were nowhere to be found. They could have been eaten by mice, stolen by the odd plumber or electrician who appeared to spend forever in the loft when trying to trace a problem or, more likely I suspect, distributed widely at my son's school over a period of time. If so, I still had no participation in the sale proceeds. A mystery indeed.

Was I angry at myself for leaving temptation in a teenager's way or proud of the early signs of my offspring's entrepreneurial acumen? I will leave you to decide but as I never broached the subject with James after such a long period, it might be that I'm doing him a deep injustice.

CHAPTER 19

ME AND MY SILLY CARS

I have always loved cars and indeed, one of my earliest memories was being given an electric plastic model of a Ford Consul when I was about four years old. At seven I was the proud owner of a Dinky Toy Rolls-Royce Silver Cloud, one of the most attractive and elegant cars ever made, and when I was ten, I bought an Airfix model of a 1927 Bentley Le Mans. This I adapted to take a battery under the bonnet, a small electric motor under the tonneau cover and by rotating the spare wheel, provided the switch. It would be four decades before I would be the proud owner of a real one.

While still at college I bought a 1948 Standard 8 tourer for £10 and later, a 1949 split-windscreen Morris Minor convertible – although it lacked a hood and had more fibreglass filler than a small boat. That was followed by a Riley 1.5, a Triumph 1300 and the bigger Triumph 2000 until I eventually owned my first Austin Mini Cooper, at the time one of the most fun cars on the market within my price range.

In the early days, being an estate agent meant that I needed to drive a four-seater car in order to accompany potential purchasers on viewings. The Austin A40 was the perfect vehicle for the job as it was one of the first hatchbacks and ideal for carrying for sale and sold boards.

I drove them all as if I was taking part in a rally and with scant regard for speed limits, which put me almost on Christian-name terms with every traffic cop around Maidstone and Tonbridge.

Then came family life, which meant I needed an estate car that could take both a pram and boards, so I had two Fiat 124 estates in a row. Company cars are not renowned for style or performance, but when I opened an office in Hythe in 1973, the Fiat 124 was soon changed to a Volvo 240 estate, followed by five Saabs in succession. These I bought from Seabrook Garage, run by Bob Allen, one of the most professional and gentlemanly dealers I have had the privilege to buy from over many years. It had always been a bit embarrassing when I parked outside a terraced house I was selling and the Volvo estate was longer than the frontage.

The Saab, however, was a classless car and ideal for the job – it was like a BMW to a BMW driver and a Ford Consul to a Ford Consul driver and at the time, the Saab 900 Turbo was the fastest production saloon on the market. After the first two Saabs, I test-drove the new Turbo model, but Sue wasn't happy with me buying one as it was unbelievably fast and 'I was quite quick enough already,' apparently! It took me two years to convince her that it really was the next car for me.

It was not until I was fifty that I felt comfortable enough to fully indulge in my passion. The business was now established and I wouldn't need to finance the acquisition of my first special car, so I went up to London and bought a 1973 Rolls-Royce Corniche fixed head coupé in dark blue. The phrase 'If it looks too good to be true then it probably is' should really have sprung to mind, but it looked so stunning in the saleroom that I just fell for it. When I got it home it stayed in the garage for three months because I was too embarrassed to be seen out in it, until Sue finally convinced me that the only people who wouldn't like it were jealous and therefore didn't need considering.

Ten members of the Maidstone Club and I set off to Calais for lunch. I took the Corniche on its first outing and after reaching the other side, the brakes overheated. It was a slow journey back as I nursed the car home. When I rang the dealer on my return, he told me to bring the car to London and he would sort it, but by then the brakes were so bad I decided to transport it up there. George, a farmer friend whose land adjoins Bitford, lent me one of his trailers and the car was loaded on by his son Stephen. The wheelbase only just fitted on the platform with a huge overhang at the rear. I sought assurance that it wouldn't fall off and was told that I could turn it over and it would still stay intact. And how right Stephen was. At 8.30am one Saturday morning I left with my precious load and after no more than ten miles on the M20, the trailer snaked and eventually turned turtle in the middle lane. Luckily, the Range Rover stayed upright but we were now astride two of the three lanes. Not a safe place to park and the Rolls was still on its roof. I put the tow car into low gear and dragged the whole sorry mess to the hard shoulder and rang 999 to advise them of the position.

I then phoned Sue – amazing how soon a 'friend' had rung her to ask if I was OK – and a fire engine arrived first, followed by an ambulance and finally the police. The traffic officer asked if I had the Range Rover handbook so he could check the towing weight, as it looked like 'an accident waiting to 'appen.' The fireman asked if I had not suffered enough, to which the policeman agreed and went off to close the motorway for an hour.

When the recovery truck arrived the owner driver, who I knew, said he would have taken the car to London for £80.

'So why are you charging me £400 to move it now?' I asked.

Apparently, it was urgent, but I was in no hurry, my day was now my own. There was more fibreglass filler on the motorway than metal.

After the car and trailer were finally loaded onto the recovery truck, the policeman gave me a five-minute start from the madding crowd of held-up motorists. All I remember is the throng of motorcycles swarming past the Range Rover as they had, of course, moved through the stationary traffic to the front of the queue.

I went to a dinner party at farmer George's house that evening to find the buns on the side plates upturned as he thought I preferred my rolls to be upside down. It was an expensive morning. I wrote off the Rolls, the Range Rover and the trailer.

I replaced the Corniche with a green Rolls-Royce Silver Spur. On its first outing I took it to France for lunch with friends. At the tunnel we were told we should really wait for the next train home, but as it was such a lovely car, they could just fit it on. During the journey under the channel my friends were fiddling with all the knobs to see what each of them did.

When we arrived in Cheriton the car wouldn't start. The tow truck was summoned and I was reminded that the train was a third of a mile long and reversing the truck all that way would hurt the driver's neck. Furthermore, as a Rolls Royce never breaks down, there is no tow hook. He eventually got the car attached and pulled it off the shuttle. On the platform the driver said he would jump-start the battery, so he took all the wine from the boot and attached two of the thickest jump leads I have ever seen – they transfer electricity from England to France using thinner cables.

The car burst into life, at which point he then put everything neatly back in the boot, despite his stiff neck. To my embarrassment all I had in sterling was a fiver, which I offered to the driver as a tip. He looked at the Rolls, then looked at me and back at the Rolls, finally asking, 'Was you wanting change?' I would like to say that was the only problem with the Spur, but sadly not.

It was 14 February and I took Sue to the Maidstone Club for a special Valentine's dinner in the Rolls. After the dinner, the car went about 500 yards before stopping – luckily out of view of most of the other members on their way home. I called the RAC, who were forty-five minutes away. As the engine wasn't working there was of course no heating, so I suggested that Sue got a taxi back home, but she said that as it was only forty-five minutes, she might as well wait.

Parked in a dark side street in a Rolls-Royce at pub chucking-out time is not the most relaxing place to be and we were grateful that a police car waited in a car park a few yards away to keep an eye on us. Unfortunately, it was a fuel pump problem and the car had to be put on a lorry as part of the relay service. The truck would be with us in forty-five minutes. Again, I suggested to Sue that as she was getting cold, she should get a taxi but as before, she said as it was only forty-five minutes she might as well wait.

When the truck arrived, it parked behind the car, which wasn't a good sign. The driver came up to say that nobody had told him it was a Rolls-Royce and the overhang at the back was too long to load onto his truck, so he would have to call a flatbed recovery vehicle. It was only forty-five minutes away.

By the time it arrived we were both freezing cold, having been sitting in an unheated car for more than two hours. The driver sat us both in his heated cab while he loaded the car and drove us back to Monks Horton. By the time we arrived home at 3.30am my plans for a romantic Valentine's night were well and truly kiboshed.

I had always wanted an E-Type Jaguar but was disappointed when I test drove a recently restored model. I agree with Enzo Ferrari that it is the most beautiful-looking sports car ever built, but the gearbox was far from smooth and getting in and out for an unathletic, big-boned fifty-seven-year-old was a challenge. I did, however, move on from thoughts of buying a Jag when I went to Sargeants of Goudhurst and spotted a low-mileage Rolls-Royce Corniche convertible in dark blue on the forecourt – and it was only a little more expensive than the E Type. Sargeants' reputation was legendary and they specialised in Rolls-Royce and Bentleys. A car bought from them would be faultless.

Over the next fifteen years the car brought Sue and me immense pleasure. We went on a charity tour to Monte Carlo and on various other tours in France and the UK with the Rolls-Royce Enthusiasts Club. Every year the south-east region of the RREC held a prizegiving picnic, which from 2010 to 2012 we hosted in our field at Bitford. The Corniche won first prize in 2015 at Aylesford Priory.

When taking the car to Brooklands with the President of the Castle Club as my passenger, the engine overheated from being stuck in traffic due to Operation Stack. The car was transported to the workshop that looks after my special vehicles. On arrival the garage owner, Alan, told the truck driver to winch it off as there were no brakes if the engine wasn't running.

The driver misheard and removed the winch, allowing the car to roll back off the lorry, gathering speed down the yard until it was stopped by a 40ft container. The car was badly damaged but when repaired it was in concourse condition. I like to drive my cars and took the view that it was as good as it would ever be and that we had satisfied all our ambitions with it, so sold it to a London buyer at a good price.

In 2004 I was at the Goodwood Revival when I saw the car of my dreams on the Racing Green Engineering stand. All the cars were built on what is called a nut and bolt restoration from chassis upwards and there was a waiting list of three years to obtain one. For a deposit of £10,000 the price was fixed, and stage payments wouldn't start until the project got underway.

With inflation higher than interest rates, I thought it would be a good idea to reserve the car and then sell it on at a profit soon after delivery. In 2007 I got the call from Peris Edwards, who ran the business, to say that the car was ready for inspection at his premises in Wales. Sue and I decided to make a weekend of it. The car was under a bespoke cover and when it was removed it looked spectacular in British racing green – beyond my wildest dreams. Sue gave me a knowing look; that car was going nowhere apart from one of my garages.

We called the Le Mans Big Bertha and it gave me enormous pleasure for the next eleven years. During that time, it went to Monte Carlo, several track days at Goodwood and Anglesey and the Le Mans Revival, where I drove her round the track with the Bentley Drivers Club.

My cars were becoming so popular for friends' weddings that Sue and I formed a partnership to promote wedding hire under the Car Men Rollers banner. We increased the fleet to include a 1989 Bentley Olympian (one of just four made) and a Rolls-Royce Silver Spur, which was a long-wheel base saloon in the same style and colour as the Corniche. We eventually sold the car to a good friend, George, for his year in office as High Sheriff.

Over the years I also bought a number of other cars including a 1937 Morris 8 Tourer, but with an 850cc side-valve engine and a top speed of 45mph, the novelty soon wore off. A replica D type Jaguar which I bought on impulse at an auction was a mistake – when I went to collect it I could not get into the driving seat so James had to drive it home until I sold it on at a modest profit.

The rarest car I bought was stretch ten- seater Range Rover, reputedly built for the Sultan of Brunei. I saw it advertised in a magazine and bought it blind. I collected it from outside Charing Cross station on the way to a black-tie do at the House of Commons. I took Barry with me and when we turned on the blower-heater we were both covered in dust and leaves from where it had been stored in a field for many months. The family hated the car, but it was great for transporting copious bridesmaids to various weddings. We also took it skiing to Courchevel – the cheapest way to travel with eight people sharing the cost.

Personalised number plates often go with a car collection and my first acquisition was CRE 1, which I bought with the proceeds of the sale of my car to Ward & Partners in 1983. Back then, £3,500 seemed a lot of money, but it has proved a good investment – not that I shall ever sell it. I also have A1 CRE, CEM50N, SEM5ON and AUC10N.

Sue, understandably, was not that keen on Big Bertha; with no roof, no windows, no heater, no radio and uncomfortable racing seats, it was an enthusiast's car but far from relaxing. By 2018, having done all that I wanted to with Big Bertha it was time to move her on. As a replacement I bought a 1964 Bentley S3, similar in shape and style to the Rolls Royce Silver Cloud which was my pride and joy when I was seven years old. Sue loved the new car with its heater and radio, and it was the one we took to the Palace in 2019.

I have to say that Sue was never at all that interested in the cars but humoured me when I wanted to take one out and, apart from the Corniche convertible, tolerated rather than enjoyed the experience until the S3 came along.

CHAPTER 20

SPORTS

Apart from cricket, where I scored for the Mote and was a member of Chart Sutton Cricket Club, either batting or as wicket keeper, team sports have never really appealed to me. Perhaps I am too impatient and like to get on with it instead of watching ten or fourteen others play while waiting to get the ball.

I was a member of the Maidstone Hockey Club in the early days and went on the Easter tours to Weymouth and Lowestoft, but usually as twelfth man or baggage handler – my expertise being driving and drinking, albeit not at the same time.

I watch very little sport, I suppose I see it as a bit like sex – wonderful to take part in but watching others perform, not quite so much fun.

At school I spent a lot of time on the fives court and in my late teens this passion transferred to the squash court. I was quite fit and fast in those days and played at least three times a week and every Sunday morning at the Maidstone Squash Club. I think what I liked about it most was that you win or fall by your own actions and that the game lasts just forty strenuous minutes. Mrs Emberson, the steward's wife, provided good home cooking in the bar after the game for a mere £1 a head. After we moved to Folkestone, I became a member of the Hythe Cricket Club, which had two new squash courts.

When I was in my fifties, I bumped into Richard, with whom I'd played every Sunday morning thirty years earlier, and suggested we have a game for old times' sake. Sue thought it a really bad idea; apparently people my age and shape die in the changing rooms. When I got back home dripping with sweat, she asked me why on earth hadn't I showered at the club, to which I replied, 'No way was I going into those changing rooms where people of my age and size die.'

Sue was remarkably patient when confronted with such logic.

Later I concentrated on tennis and for the next twenty-five years played a men's foursome at Bitford every Tuesday evening and Sunday morning. For the teams involved there were no excuses for not attending and if there was a conflicting appointment, a substitute was always keen to join us. After the Tuesday games we would enjoy a supper that Sue had prepared and put the world to rights over a couple of bottles of wine and the odd glass of whisky, often into the early hours. Sadly, age and injuries from skiing took their toll and those wonderful times are now no more than a memory.

However, the loss of tennis was compensated by being asked to join the local farmers' Wednesday night boys' evening, which started with bowls followed by steak and chips at a local hostelry and then back to one of the members' houses for snooker. In 2019 the bowls was dropped as we had increasing difficulty bending down to pick up the woods. The meal and snooker, I am pleased to say, continues to this day.

When I was younger, I tried my hand at golf but found it difficult to justify the time away from the office during the week and Sundays were always family days if I wasn't working. When I was elevated to the Prudential Regional ivory tower in Maidstone, it was the first time in my career that my office was closed at weekends. The children were older by then and Sue had already planned her Saturday mornings for the past twenty-five years, so suggested I take up golf again.

I played at the recently opened Weald of Kent course, but still to this day my golf isn't great, although I do enjoy the camaraderie. Sport to me is more about the people than the game itself. Since 2012 I have arranged a golf tour for eight to twelve players to Spain in the spring and autumn – any more players complicates restaurant bookings, tee times and transport.

We stay in frontline villas with separate en-suite rooms. I think we have all got to an age where sharing sleeping accommodation is neither healthy nor desirable. If it wasn't for the golf, these trips would be even better. The bar bills are more expensive than the food and we have always enjoyed a good mix of players with handicaps from two to twenty-six. The problem these days, as we have more time in retirement, is to limit the numbers to a manageable level.

I came to skiing late in life but when James was ten it seemed a good thing to learn together. Sue was not keen and Becky thought it was dangerous so preferred to stay at home and ride her horse, which I reckoned was even more risky.

The learning bit and bonding didn't go too well – James was skiing off piste within three days while I was still making a fool of myself on the nursery slopes. However, I have skied almost every year since then, apart from a short break during the property recession of 1989-1993.

In 1994 my friend David Apthorp, a professional events organiser, invited me to join a trip he was arranging for about twenty-five to thirty people to the Hotel Floride in Courchevel 1650. It was an amazing experience and a fabulous mix of husbands and wives, fathers and sons, families and courting couples, our ages ranging from five to sixty-five. James and I joined the party for the next four years, at which time David decided it had run its course.

As you may have guessed by now, there is nothing I like more than organising trips so, with David's blessing, I took over the planning side and we subsequently moved upmarket to the Le Portetta, a superb ski-in, ski-out four-star hotel with its own spa and excellent restaurant. There were even people to help you put on your warmed boots in the morning – such luxury.

At first I would reserve the whole hotel and fill the rooms with friends and their friends. One year there were complaints that either the rooms were not piste facing, had no balcony or were twin and not double and vice versa.

Why I didn't think of it years before I'm not sure, but the following year I agreed the 'Emson special deal and week' with the hotel, then emailed everyone to tell them when it was and that if they wanted to join the party, to book their room direct with the Le Portetta. This would also mean that their credit card insurance would be valid if they needed to claim and that any problems from then on would be between the hotel and their guest. Job done.

Some of the original team still go there to this day, but a couple of new hips prevented me from skiing for three years.

I am not the first to comment that I enjoy organising trips, lunches and parties if only to make sure I am included. Despite being less than average in all the sports I play, they have given me enormous pleasure over the years and enabled me to meet some really interesting people, many of whom have become good friends.

CHAPTER 21

CLUBS AND SOCIETIES

Over the years I have belonged to many clubs and societies, which has given me the chance to meet like-minded people with similar interests, whether that be cars, sport, charity, dining or business. Some I have been deeply involved with, others not so much; the common thread is that I am usually called on for help with fundraising auctions or after-dinner speeches.

Most come with memories, some good, some not so good, but all have proved stimulating at the time. Added together, that's nearly thirty different organisations, placed here in alphabetical order so as not to offend anyone and ranging from the famous to others you will probably never have heard of.

Falling into the latter category is the Almost Modern Order of Purchasers (known as the Purchasers), a club comprising a brotherhood of all men of good repute who 'had made a damn stupid mistake, been badly done to, or lived lives of crass buffoonery.' When nominated, I qualified on all three counts. The dinners and cricket matches are held for fun, but also contribute much-needed funds to local charities.

My love of cars is well known and I joined the Bentley Drivers Club when I bought my first Bentley in 2007. The club holds rallies and meetings in prestigious locations, one of the most memorable being when I took part in a parade of Bentleys invited to enter the keep at the Tower of London to watch the Ceremony of the Keys, followed by a tour and brilliant buffet in the Beefeaters' private club quarters. The Club also arranges dinners and meets at prestigious venues around the country during the year.

Brooklands Museum is a very special place for motoring enthusiasts, on the site of the world's first purpose-built racing circuit and home to an impressive display of vintage racing cars, planes and buses. I conduct the auction at the annual dinner to raise funds for the charity. Until his death in 2020 Stirling Moss was president and attended most annual dinners; a charming and lovely man. One of my best memories was the dinner held to celebrate the golden anniversary of Concorde, when the nose was raised and lowered, a rare occurrence.

I enjoy golf and am a member of both Littlestone and Boughton Golf Clubs. Etchinghill Golf Club is affiliated to Boughton where between eight and twelve of us meet to play every week, followed by the mandatory lunch and repartee. Many of the Tuesday morning team are part of the Spanish tours and it is also where my grandson Charlie is learning the skill of the game, with the help of the talented pro, Ollie.

I was invited to join the Castle Club when I became President of the Old Roffensian Society in 2006. One of the UK's few remaining gentlemen's dining clubs (although they let me in), themed monthly dinners are held and once a year I host the Auctioneer's Dinner. Traditional standards are strictly maintained; a member would not enter the premises, even to deliver a letter, unless he was wearing a tie and however hot the weather, jackets are never removed at the dining table. The beautiful period building where we meet is owned by the members and overlooks the River Medway at Rochester.

The highlight of the year for me is the Boys' Toys Day, where we all take our special or classic cars and drive to a secret venue for lunch. One year I arranged a visit to the members' private dining room at Brooklands for sixty-five of us; unfortunately, my car, with the president in the passenger seat, broke down on the way. I am a director on the board which is responsible for the smooth running of the club.

The Castle Club is affiliated to the Savile Club in Brook Street, Mayfair where Sue, Becky, Livvy and I stayed the night before our trip to the Palace. It is also an excellent place to meet friends in London for lunch or dinner.

I became a Friend of Rochester Cathedral after sitting next to the Dean, Adrian Newman, at my first Old Roffensian Dinner as president, held at Leeds Castle. Until then I had forgotten (or probably not appreciated when I was younger) just what a special place the cathedral is. As a company we have sponsored many events there, including a visit by the London Welsh Male Voice Choir when the singing accompanied by the wonderful organ was a rendition to remember. The dinners in the crypt, which I initiated for the Old Roffensian Dinner, provide a superb setting for fundraising events. I am also a founder member of the Gundulf Society, which supports the cathedral.

Firmly linking my interest in cars and fundraising for charitable causes, especially when they involve young people, the Full Monty Charity evolved out of tragedy. A young student at Kent College died of cancer and his brother David decided to do something positive by generating an income for the Teenage Cancer Trust. Brought together by our love of cars, the business plan was to arrange a trip for twenty-five supercars, each with two occupants, to drive to Monte Carlo, staying at top hotels and eating in Michelin-star restaurants on the way. The cost per head was £1,500, so we had £75,000 in the kitty for the event.

Steve Hamilton, one of the parents at the school, headed up the trip with the help of David's parents and negotiated special deals for the supercars. He managed to buy £75,000-worth of hospitality, with discounts, for £60,000, giving us a surplus of £15,000 before we had even left the UK. With raffles, fines and the obligatory auction at the Café de Paris, the venture raised £25,000.

For our first year I took Sue in the Rolls Royce Corniche and for the second year I went in the Bentley Le Mans with my co-driver, Chris, a farmer with knowledge of how engines work and slightly more likely than Sue to get under the car if there was a problem. We were told when presenting the cheque to the Teenage Cancer Trust that we had used the wrong logo and not to do it again without committee approval. The third year we made similar money, but this time for our own charity, the Kent Young People's Fund, which still exists to this day.

Goodwood Road Racing Club, run by Viscount Richmond (formerly Lord March) is the epitome of quality and high standards and shows that there are still people happy to pay for excellence rather than try to trim everything to the lowest possible price, sacrificing standards on the way.

There are three main meetings for the GRRC – a member's meeting, The Festival of Speed and the Revival – all held around the Goodwood motor racetrack. It was here that I first met Peris of Racing Green Engineering, from whom I bought my Bentley Le Mans. As a member of the GRRC I attend at least two or three track days a year and at one of those I was invited to join OF Racing Club. A retired builder friend of mine from Folkestone often flies me to the meetings in his helicopter, a real treat compared to queuing for ages at the car parks.

I was honoured to be invited to join the Kent Ambassadors, a select group of highly successful and experienced people who either work or live in Kent and have come together voluntarily to help all aspects of life in the county. I have met some remarkable people at the briefings and it's given me the opportunity to open a few doors in walls that I didn't know existed, including meeting the Lord Lieutenant at one event and persuading him to open a new care home in Gravesend for one of my friend's charities, Abbeyfield Kent (now rebranded as Rapport).

It was an £8.5 million development, part of which was on land we had sold to them at auction, and the CEO, Leon, was struggling to get someone of note to perform the ceremony. I also met and became a friend of Sir Robert Worcester who, many years later, allowed my charity, Young Lives Foundation, to celebrate its 10th anniversary in the great hall at his home, Allington Castle.

I have always had an interest in cricket and there can be few better ways of spending a sunny afternoon than sitting around the county ground in Canterbury hearing the contact between leather and willow. As a member of Kent County Cricket Club, I have filled many marquees with friends and business associates over the years, both at Maidstone and Canterbury and it's a setting and atmosphere that always ensures success.

Sadly, in recent years my energies have been diverted elsewhere since much of the land around the Canterbury ground has been sold for development and only a few marquees remain. Parking on site has been seriously reduced and unfortunately, park and ride has never really appealed to me.

I did suggest to the chairman that they should sell all the land and create a new venue in a rural location where land values are considerably less. He told me that they couldn't do that as they owned the ground; an illusion indeed as with the overdraft at the time they actually owned very little of it.

The other problem was that they had franchised the catering to an outside company who had paid a hefty premium for the privilege. Naturally, the company had to recoup their investment, so no food was allowed in the ground unless provided by the franchisee. It was on the face of it a good deal, as the club was losing around £20,000 in catering fees and the premium for the licence was at a similar amount, meaning they were £40,000 up. However, that's also a sum quickly eroded if you can't get the spectators through the gates.

Although I don't like the atmosphere of the Twenty20 matches, they do provide the revenue to pay the shortfall in staging the traditional matches. As is so often the case, it's more about money than the sport, or perhaps I am just being old-fashioned in trying to preserve a tradition beyond its sell-by date.

To qualify for membership of the Kent Hoppers Tie Club you must be male, over twenty-one and connected with Kent either by birth, marriage or residence. All nominations have to be proposed by a member who has played cricket for Kent. My proposer was Brian Luckhurst and seconder John Shepherd. The club holds bi-annual lunches and attracts illustrious speakers of the calibre of Sir Gary Sobers and Sir John Major. There is also an annual golf day and dinner held at Belmont and it is one of the few marquees at the St Lawrence Ground during cricket week. Members are also obliged to wear the Hoppers club tie on Mondays.

I joined the Lord's Taverners in 1989, becoming chairman and subsequently president of the East Kent Branch. The summer ball, cricket day and Christmas lunch regularly raised £30,000 a year, enough to buy one of the legendary green buses for local charities.

My father was president of Maidstone Club in 1982 and introduced me as a member in the 1970s. It was a gentleman's club, similar to the Castle Club, although towards the end it did, after much debate, allow women members – although ironically none wanted to join. I was elected president in 1996 and when I took on the role of chairman in 2010-12, I did feel that the club was an anachronism and really needed dragging into the 20th century.

The management board of fifteen looked after eighty-five members, two part-time staff and a turnover of below £80,000 a year. I tried but failed to slim down the board to six, but with no hope of a decision ever being made, I resigned as chairman, though still attending on a regular basis until the club was closed and the building sold in 2016. Many of the members still meet once a quarter at Frederic Bistro in Maidstone.

I am a vice-president of Mersham-le-Hatch Cricket Club, which has the most delightful village ground where HRH Prince Philip was a regular player in the days when Lord Brabourne owned the estate. The house and grounds are now owned by good friends of mine and the two brothers, Jeremy and Jordan, work tirelessly to keep the teams and games played on a regular basis.

I joined the National Association of Estate Agents, our professional body, in the late 1960s and served over the years as both chairman and president of the East Kent Branch. I represented the association on the NAEA/RICS joint committee and for the first time, managed to get the auction steering committee for both organisations working together. I was elected to the College of Fellows in recognition of my 'signal service' to the NAEA in the 1980s

The National Association of Valuers and Auctioneers was the auctioneering arm of the NAEA and I was a founder member. The whole organisation is now under the Propertymark banner and James is very involved at national level, having been on the committee since 2010 and chairman in 2018/20. He now represents the association on the joint RICS liaison Committee.

I was introduced to Freemasonry in 1989. My father had been an active Freemason but wasn't the one to recommend me to the brotherhood. I enjoyed the fellowship, the festive boards (their name for the dinner) but really struggled with the formal part of the proceedings.

As a recognised after-dinner speaker I was expected to be good at the oratory, but being dyslexic I found learning the pages of ritual almost impossible and couldn't understand why successful businessmen were reduced to quivering wrecks trying to remember their lines, hampered by stage whispers every time they stumbled. I had just started the new business and decided that this was an extra pressure I really did not need, so reluctantly resigned –to the eternal disappointment of my proposer.

OF Racing stands for Old Farts and is a club for former racing drivers, mechanics and related connections to motorsport. The strapline is 'the older we get, the faster we were' – how very true. The President, until his death, was Sir Stirling Moss. The Club arranges track days and tours in France, Wales and the UK. Once again, I am the unofficial auctioneer, selling all manner of memorabilia when asked at the various dinners.

The Old Roffensian Society is open to former students and staff of King's School, Rochester and I have been a member since leaving the school in 1962, becoming president in 2006-9. It was a great opportunity to re-engage with the school and the cathedral following four decades in the wilderness.

Membership of the Rolls-Royce Enthusiasts Club is open to owners and admirers of the eponymous marque. I joined when I bought my first Rolls-Royce Corniche in 2005 and hosted the south-east section prize-giving days at Bitford for three consecutive years. Sue and I also enjoyed European tours, ably organised by the chairman Stephen and his partner Len. I got to meet a number of interesting characters, including Richard, who has become a good friend, owns a most magnificent and rare collection of

Rolls-Royce cars and lives no more than two miles from my home.

I first joined Hythe Rotary in the early 1970s, transferring to Maidstone in the late 1980s. It is a truly magnificent international organisation whose members work tirelessly for the local and wider community. Although no longer a member, I still support many of the Kent clubs with charity auctions and after-dinner speaking engagements. I have also accepted an invitation to speak at the regional conference on two occasions. YLF was, through my introduction, charity of the year for the south-east region, which was quite an accolade.

Round Table was my first introduction to and experience of charity work. I felt very privileged to be introduced by John Heddle in the late 1960s. A rule of becoming a member is that only one representative of any profession is allowed to join a club. Folkestone already had an estate agent, surveyor and auctioneer within the membership, so I was invited to be a founder member of the new Romney Marsh Round Table.

I enjoyed the meetings and the repartee and found it a welcome change from the pressures of running a new estate agency business. However, when I then opened offices in Dymchurch, New Romney and Lydd, after five years nearly every member was a client and the meetings became more about house sales than enjoyment, so when the opportunity presented itself, I transferred to Folkestone and District Round Table.

I was one of a team of three who won the regional debating competition three years running, became chairman in 1983 and president during the year Folkestone hosted the national conference, where 10,000 Tablers descended on the coastal town. Many of the people I met through Round Table have been close friends for forty years or more.

I was honoured to be elected as a Fellow of the Royal Institution of Chartered Surveyors in recognition of my services to auctioneering and the work I contributed to the joint NAVA/RICS committee which pioneered the common auction conditions of sale now adopted by both organisations and widely used throughout the profession.

The Stone Street Club is a social club in the heart of Maidstone where many of the lunchtime members of Maidstone Club decamped on its demise and is still a comfortable place to catch up with fellow businessmen in the town.

The Wooden Spoon Club is the rugby equivalent of the Taverners and I have conducted many auctions for the club since becoming a member, but never really got involved with the running of a branch.

The Worshipful Company of Fruiterers is a progressive City livery company that has been actively supporting the City of London and the fruit industry since the 13th century. On election to the Freedom of the Company, the Freeman also obtains the Freedom of the City of London. If only I had sheep to drive over London Bridge! I was proposed by my farmer friend Chris after a banquet at the Mansion House as I already knew a number of the members, either through the business, other clubs or classic car rallies.

Being a member of so many wonderful organisations has been a privilege and I have really enjoyed meeting so many varied people from all walks of life, many of whom have become lifelong loyal friends.

CHAPTER 22

AFTER-DINNER SPEAKING

There can be few better sounds than those of an audience laughing at a story or joke during an after-dinner speech

My public speaking started with Round Table, where I was part of a debating team either supporting or opposing a motion set by the host table, who then judged the best and most persuasive arguments. Dennis would set the scene for the first twelve minutes and following the opener for the opposition, Tony or Chris would take the next eight minutes.

My five-minute role was to round up the debate, taking into account all that had been said from both sides. This was mainly ad lib, but I did have some standard notes in reserve, often finishing on the bell with the phrase – when there is no more to be said, some bloody fool will stand up and say it – 'Over to you, Mr Wind-upper for the opposition!'

I have been addressing audiences for more than four decades, starting with small gatherings such as Rotary or Round Table Ladies Circle and moving on to prestigious dinners attended by hundreds of guests.

Most are relatively straightforward; I have many subjects and experiences to draw on and adapt as I go along to suit the listeners. This is one advantage of speaking without notes, although there are inevitable dangers with such an approach.

Tailoring the speech to the audience is essential – I never swear when ladies are present but at rugby club or golf days there are few limits to the depths one can plunge to get a laugh.

I was talking to a ladies' lunch club in Thanet and decided to recall some stories from my furniture auction days, to which most of them could relate. Part of the routine was referring to the archetypal dealers in the 1970s and 80s, who always drove Volvo Estate cars with large roof racks. I was halfway through recounting that many had ponytails which, whether on a horse or a human, when you lifted it up there was an enormous…then I remembered the totally inappropriate punchline, and hastily changed it to 'an enormous backside underneath.' At which point a lady from the back piped up, 'When my husband told me that joke, he said "arsehole"', which brought a greater laugh than I could have expected as the ladies realised the predicament I had tried to avoid.

As a vice president of the Folkestone Rugby Club, I was asked to do the pre-match speech between the lunch and the start of the game. It was an all-male event, with many liberally imbibed before I stood up. The jokes became more and more vulgar as the raucous laughter encouraged me to dig even deeper into the Anglo-Saxon vocabulary where no word or phrase was out of bounds.

As I came to the end, the curtain at the back of the dining room was drawn back to reveal a cluster of ladies who had prepared the meal and were now ready to serve the coffee.

They would have heard the whole speech. I was devastated and apologised profusely to them, but with good grace they said it was not a problem – they were used to such language – which was very sweet of them, but I still felt uncomfortable

As with everything, I tend not to dwell on the successes but to try to analyse the ones that did not go too well – and there have been a few!

The Brighton and Hove Estate Agents annual dinner is a popular evening attended by 350-400 members and their guests and held in the main ball room of the Grand Hotel on the seafront. In 2001, I was invited to speak at the event, and it was a disaster. The public address system wasn't functioning properly, so the guests around the perimeters of the room couldn't hear me and instead started talking among themselves. As their conversation became more animated, the tables next to them were also struggling to hear and so they started talking. For the first time in my experience, I had completely lost the room and was effectively just talking to a handful of tables directly in front of the podium. After a while I said to the small group, 'Why not join me in the bar and I'll tell you the rest there?' On the way home I have never felt so dejected and considered making that my last appearance.

I seldom have nerves before public speaking, but I did feel some apprehension when asked by a good friend of mine, John Oakley, President of the Toastmasters Guild, to speak at their annual dinner in London. The audience would have heard the very best and the very worst of guest speakers and no doubt every joke both recent and traditional that had ever been delivered. I decided to concentrate on personal experiences, which they would not have heard before, usually ending with me being the butt of the joke. Timing is everything and the sound of laughter confirmed that I had pitched it right for the occasion.

Law Society dinners are often a challenge, as the audience ranges from humorous young lawyers to the staider senior practitioners and High Court judges. At the Bromley Law Society Annual Dinner in 1992, there was an area in the room that was notably unresponsive, something that can be quite off-putting to the speaker.

My theme for the evening had been the failure of the Prudential in their attempt to modernise the estate agency profession, resulting in a reported loss of some £400 million in just three years. Corporate speak was always good for a laugh, including phrases such as 'Clive, have you a window in your diary?', to which the response was, 'Since you took over I haven't even got a window in my office." Or 'open seven days a week' was not an advert – more a boast that they were in it for the long term.

After the formal proceedings, one of the party from the unresponsive table came up and introduced himself as the senior solicitor at the Pru, who had been invited by one of the local firms of solicitors. Naturally, they were embarrassed that I was taking the mickey out of one of their invitees. I made some glib comment that whenever I spoke on that theme there was always someone present who claimed to work for the Pru in Holborn, but when he mentioned his name, it certainly rang a bell.

'Can I expect a writ?" I asked, to which the answer was:

'Of course not – all that you said was indeed true!'

One of my most memorable evenings was at the United Reformed Church hall in my hometown of Hythe, where I was asked to address the Hythe Conservation Society. The audience was packed with friends and acquaintances I had known for twenty-five years and I was able to pick out many faces and recount an amusing story about each of them. Although my spot was for thirty minutes, I was still keeping them amused for well over an hour and a half and was asked to stay on for a bit longer as I brought the session to a close. A wonderful evening enjoyed by all.

On several occasions I have been asked to step in at the last minute after the chosen speaker has cried off due to illness or transport problems. One such time I received a call from the secretary at Rochester Cathedral at 4pm to ask if I could speak for ten minutes at the dinner in the crypt that evening attended by 100 guests.

'Sorry, Lynne, I can't do that," I replied. '

'But you are coming aren't you?" she asked.

'Yes, I will be there – I can do thirty to-forty minutes but ten will be too short to engage the audience and make any impression!"

I spent the evening next to the Bishop and Dean and managed to pitch the address without offending anybody while keeping the audience amused in spectacular surroundings.

On another occasion I received a call in my car at 4.30 asking me to step into the breach that evening – I had nothing planned, so I agreed. The young daughter of a close friend was in the front seat as I was doing the school run that day.

'Gosh,' she said, 'they must be desperate.'

To her embarrassment I replied, 'Well, I'm not that bad at it.' – a joke we have shared over the years.

As with most things, the more you do the better it gets – adding a few extra embellishments to tried and tested routines and venturing off-piste if the audience is receptive to a particular theme can pay dividends.

Sadly, the Covid pandemic curtailed all engagements for eighteen months but no doubt normal service will be resumed in time.

CHAPTER 23

COURT CASES AND THE LAW

If I had been blessed with an academic brain, I have no doubt that I would have become a lawyer. Courts, like auction rooms, are perfect stages for the theatrically minded and I realise now that justice and the law courts are often some distance apart.

Since 1989, when we founded Clive Emson Auctioneers, I have represented the company in the county court for ten of the twelve cases we have brought in the last thirty-two years.

The first time we sued a client for non-payment of fees, the solicitor charged £600 but the judge awarded us just £250 costs, a shortfall of £350. After that I decided I could represent the company on straightforward cases.

Little did I realise that my first appearance, one very hot Friday afternoon, would provide the judge with quite a bit of amusement. It had taken six months to get the case to this stage and just five minutes before the trial, I was handed a piece of paper by the clerk of the court stating that I could not represent a limited company without a lawyer present, unless given leave to by the judge.

Before the case began, I asked the court leave to represent the company.

'Why do you not have a solicitor to represent you?' I was asked by the judge.

'Well, your honour,' I replied, 'it's so straightforward it would be an insult to waste the lawyer's time.'

I was greeted with a mirthful, 'Oh, Mr Emson, if only the law was that simple, I would be out of a job.'

I was then asked how I would present the evidence. I explained that I had both the contract and the email from the defendant breaking the terms by withdrawing the lot twelve hours before the auction. I was told, in a rather supercilious tone, that had I engaged a lawyer he would ask me questions in the witness box and my replies would form the evidence. I was getting quite frustrated by this point, having taken so long to get to this stage and I really didn't want the hearing to be postponed.

'How about if I stand in the box and answer the questions that a lawyer would ask me if he was here, and if I forget something, maybe you could ask me?' I suggested.

'So, you want me to cross-examine you?' asked the judge.

'Only if I forget something that my lawyer might have asked,' I said as the charade continued.

With a wry smile, the judge invited me into the witness box and proceeded with the examination. After I had finished giving my evidence, the judge asked the defendant if he had any questions for me.

'No,' came the reply. 'Mr Emson has been more than fair and honest.'

He was then asked what his defence was, to which the reply came: 'I think three per cent is too much money.'

'Do you mean the three per cent specified in Clause 2 of the contract that you signed?' asked the judge. When the defendant confirmed that to be the case, the judge looked at me and said 'I think, Mr Emson, on this basis my job could well be in jeopardy' and gave judgement in my favour.

The defendant pleaded poverty and offered £10 a month. The judge he said he was not there to negotiate the payment but from the look on my face, it might be wise to think of something slightly more tangible. In the end we settled for his daughter's Nissan Micra, which we sold in a local car auction to recover our fees.

When the next case came up some months later, I decided that I would try to avoid any further humiliation and asked my local solicitor to give me £50 of his time just to clarify the procedure, including whether I addressed the bench as your Honour, Sir or Judge.

While I was there, the solicitor asked if he could give the papers a quick look over. He then pointed out that the defendant had not put in a defence but a counterclaim and as there was no defence, I should ask for judgement immediately and then it would be up to the other party to present their case. That bit of advice was worth every penny of the £50 agreed fee.

I had already cleared with the court that I could represent my company. As we were shown into court, I was presented with my first hurdle – the judge was in fact a lady. Did I address her as Duchess? I mused to myself. The case started and as advised I asked for judgement, only to be told that the judge had already read the papers and there was a defence.

'I think you will find it is a counterclaim,' I responded with some confidence.

On re-reading the papers the judge agreed and gave me judgement. The counterclaim was thrown out as well, so a result all round. I was beginning to like my new calling!

The other cases that we brought over the years were straightforward; I would not issue a writ if all the paperwork wasn't perfect and in place. If there was any doubt whatsoever, we would not prosecute.

In one memorable hearing the client had a different recollection about events concerning the release of keys and in his summing up, the judge said that when there was such a disparity of evidence it was his duty to decide who was telling the truth. He finished by saying, 'The eye for detail, excellent record keeping and professionalism shown in all aspects of the process by the claimant leads me to believe that they are telling the truth and they would not make such a fundamental error. Accordingly, I give judgement in favour of the claimant.'

Only twice have I employed a barrister to act on behalf of the company. The first was in Tunbridge Wells County Court where we were suing for non-payment of fees amounting to £13,000. It was not the amount involved but the fact that I was told the person I was suing was a front man for a notorious property owner and landlord.

I was advised to drop the case, but that is how bullies get away with it. They owed me £13,000 and I wanted it. An attractive young female barrister was sent from a London chambers and I took to her immediately. As we were walking from the solicitor's office to the hearing, she said that she hadn't come across the barrister on the other side before, but that at fifty-eight years old and defending a £13,000 claim, he hadn't peaked yet. Just my sense of humour.

Counsel for the defence was a Rumpole-type character clearly recovering from an over-indulgence of brandy the night before. The first question my barrister put to the defendant was: 'Did you resign as a director of the company purely because you were sent to prison for two years for fraud, or were there any other reasons?'

After a moment, the judge asked the defendant's counsel if he was happy with the question, to which he sat up from his relaxed position and said, 'No – objection, your honour.'

'I should think so too. It is expunged from my mind as we speak,' said the judge, scribbling a note on his pad.

It went from bad to worse for the defendant as he tried to explain why he had changed his name twice during the transaction. The final straw came when the judge referred to two previous applications to have the case set aside, which were totally contradictory. Was that his signature on both applications, he was asked and if so, how could they be so different?

The astounding reply was that his brief had told him the first wouldn't help their case, so he'd changed it. We were given judgement with costs which were paid within forty-eight hours as the judge had made it quite clear that a further hearing would not be in the defendant's best interest. Once again, our legal fees were substantially more than those sanctioned by the court, but it was still a good result.

Our biggest case was a claim for £83,000 against BT in damages for a telephone system they sold us and installed but which was not fit for purpose. The BT site notes in our office recorded that one of their engineers stated that the system had been installed incorrectly three years earlier, but even if it had been put in properly it would still not operate as we were told.

At the first pre-trial hearing in Maidstone County Court, the young barrister sent by BT was far from competent. He asked for the case to be thrown out as there were no grounds for the claim. The judge, whom I had appeared before on several occasions, said that she had a letter with a list of ten valid concerns. Her utter frustration was hardly disguised when told that he did not have that letter in his bundle. The barrister was torn off a strip with the advice that next time he appeared he was properly briefed, and that Mr Emson was not known in this court for bringing spurious claims. A second pre-trial date was agreed for some three months later.

At that pre-trial hearing the barrister for the defence asked that as the issues were somewhat complex, he wanted a full three-day trial rather than the fast-track approach. I was asked by the judge if I was agreeable. When I said that I was, she asked if I knew what it meant.

'Yes, it means I have to waste three days rather than just one.'

Well perhaps so, I was told, but it also meant that whoever won paid all the costs for the other side. The rookie barrister was taken aback when I replied, 'Well, if they can afford it, let's get a date agreed.' Apparently, I should have given up at this stage; the costs for BT alone could be around £15-20,000.

I employed a barrister to represent the company at the hearing; with so much at stake it wasn't ideal to rely on an amateur to argue with a professional on the other side. Less than twelve hours before the hearing, BT made an offer that it would have been unwise to refuse. Even if in the right, court cases can take an unexpected outcome.

The only case that we lost was on a technicality under The Unfair Terms in Consumer Contracts Regulations 1999, where there is a provision for a fourteen-day cooling-off period if the agreement is signed on the defendant's premises. All staff know that the agreement must be returned by the client after time for due consideration of the terms has been given. In this case it wasn't until cross-examination that it emerged that one of our negotiators had dropped the contract in by hand and, trying to be helpful, waited for it to be signed as the client wasn't very mobile. As soon as I heard this, I knew we were on the back foot; the defendant wasn't aware of the impact this statement would have, but I had no doubt that the judge would be unlikely to miss it.

I think the best advice one can receive is to keep out of court if possible. The process is long-winded, expensive and however solid the case, you must always bear in mind that the other side has presumably also been advised that they have a good chance of winning the day.

I took this sage advice when I was inadvertently on the wrong side of the law. We had bought a site for a new office on the junction of the A259 and the M20. I wanted to flame gun and level the site before applying for planning, but was advised by my architect that this would irritate the planners and that being an island site surrounded by major roads, there was unlikely to be any wildlife of consequence.

Planning was granted subject to an ecology survey, which led to the discover of great crested newts. At the time they were protected by a European-initiated law under the UK Wildlife and Countryside Act 1981 as an endangered species. We employed an ecology firm to advise on their removal.

A few weeks later I received a call at the office to say that children had broken into the derelict building and were climbing over the dead trees. I engaged a contractor to fell the trees and board up the house. A few days later I got a call from the police. I had been reported by a local Liberal councillor for allowing work on a site known to be inhabited by great crested newts.

I had a laugh with my lawyer, Patrick, until he phoned back to say that we needed to take this seriously. The penalty was a fine up to £1,000 for each newt or up to six months in prison.

I was duly interviewed under caution by two officers who came to my office to record the meeting. My solicitor told me to say 'no comment' to all questions and make them prove the case. When the two policemen arrived, they had an enormous file with reports, letters and plans. I asked for five minutes with my brief in another room and told Patrick that they clearly had all the information they needed and that my 'no comment' would merely antagonise them and make me sound like a criminal. I wanted to talk my way out of this one. Patrick's advice of 'no comment' stood, but he also said I must do what I felt comfortable with.

I started by thanking them for coming to my office rather than me having to visit the police station. I went on to say that I had inspected the custody cells as part of my role as chairman of YLF, a charity that provides all the appropriate adults when required. That impressed them. They knew how valuable our volunteers are to them when vulnerable young people are arrested.

I continued by saying that I was in a dilemma as soon as I received the call about the children playing on the site. Imagine, had I ignored the call and a child was hurt, how the press would accuse me, the chairman of a children's charity, of trying to save £1,500 at the expense of endangering children. If I made the area safe, I was guilty of disturbing a protected site. I decided that the children's safety took priority over great crested newts which may be in danger in Germany, but show me any building site in Kent and I am sure there would be found great crested newts or bats, glow worms, rare orchids et al.

After discussing the matter with the Director of Public Prosecutions, the police offered me a caution to conclude the matter. I wanted to argue the point in court, but took Patrick's advice this time. I was guilty as charged – mitigation might work but with the wrong magistrate the fine could be horrendous and the local newspapers would certainly pick it up. One of the policemen said that three years earlier they would not have bothered, but with a councillor baying for blood and EU involvement, they had no option but to pursue the case. What a waste of valuable police time and all in the name of justice.

CHAPTER 24

AWARDS, ACCOLADES AND HONOURS

The work I do, whether professionally or for charity, is because I enjoy it and feel that if you're blessed with a talent, then it's a sin to waste it. My strong points are communication, auctioneering, networking and making things happen. I also have an ability to keep an audience amused and encourage young people to talk instead of relying on texting.

It is said that no good deed ever goes unpunished and public acknowledgement of any achievements is a bonus, not a right. My first awards came between 1978 and 1980 when I won the ISVA National Auctioneering Competition Rose Bowl three years in a row, an achievement only managed by two people before me, Jack Walter in the 1950s and John Heddle in the 1960s. Both men were also from the Kent branch.

My work on the joint NAVA/RICS committees - where, for the first time, both organisations were in harmony in respect of auctions and especially the Common Auction Conditions of Sale adopted by all the major UK auction houses - resulted in me being elevated to the College of Fellows at NAVA in 2005 and gaining a rare invitation to join the RICS as a Fellow member in 2010.

In 2012 I was invited to join the Kent Ambassadors, a Kent County Council-sponsored group of about seventy members, each regarded as outstanding in their own field.

Our role is to promote Kent and spread the word about organisations operating within the county.

In 2015, YLF received the Queen's Award for Voluntary Services, a national acknowledgement for the amazing work the charity has contributed to children and families in Kent, the majority of which was under my chairmanship but could not have been achieved without the dedication of CEO Stephen Gray, his team and the 250 amazing volunteers.

In 2016 I was the winner of the Outstanding Contribution to Business in Kent award by KEiBA and the following year the Kent Invicta Award presented by the chairman of KCC for my contribution to vulnerable young people in Kent.

The climax, of course, was the totally unexpected letter from the Cabinet Office informing me that I had been recommended to become a Member of the Order of the British Empire in Her Majesty the Queen's 2019 Birthday Honours List for services to vulnerable children in Kent. It was a bolt from the blue, but could not have come at a better time.

Had it not been for Sue's constant support and patience it would never have happened, and we were able to attend the ceremony at Buckingham Palace just five months before she passed away. I cannot imagine what it would have been like without her by my side on such an important occasion. I was allowed three guests, so it was not only another memorable day for both Sue and me but also Becky and Livvy, who joined us.

Epilogue

When I look back over the past seventy years or so I have tried to reflect on lessons that I may have learned on the way.

There is no doubt that if you are lucky enough to have a supportive family and close and loyal friends the journey is more likely to be a happy and rewarding one.

I am great believer that if you are not in the room, you are not in the deal. Making the effort to attend meetings, join likeminded groups and respect your colleagues, friends and clients offers untold opportunities to make things happen.

There is no doubt that I was born at the right time. I am not sure it would be possible to create a new business with financial assistance from the banks and other financial institutions. No longer do we have bank managers empowered to make decisions or use their initiative to lend to an individual without the computer ticking all the boxes.

Choosing the right partner or team is also essential to running a good business. The odd mistakes in my career have always been as much down to having the wrong partner as the decision to venture outside my area of expertise – stick to what you know has certainly worked for me.

The most important thing that I think I have learnt is that success is not measured by money or material wealth, but the behaviour and endeavours of your children and grandchildren and the loyalty of friends who are there to support you in good times and bad.

I hope you have enjoyed reading the book and my apologies to the very many friends and acquaintances if you have not been mentioned.